The Secrets

TO BEING AN
UNSTOPPABLE WOMAN

Ellen

Keep Rising!

Other books available in the Unstoppable Publishing's Library:

10 Ways to Prevent Failure (Audio Book)
A straightforward guide to help you stay focused on attaining your goals.

Starting Today
365 Quotations to stimulate, inspire, and enhance your personal growth.

The Unstoppable Woman's Guide to Emotional Well-Being
A book for women written by 23 female authors, coaches and professionals.

How to Write & Publish Your Book NOW!!
Step by step guide to put you on the fast track top becoming a published author.

Success Guide for the Unstoppable Entrepreneur
Straightforward guide to help new business owners and entrepreneurs excel in their business.

If You Leave, I Will Kill You! – Getting Off the Beaten Path of Domestic Violence

www.TheUnstoppableWoman.net

The Secrets

TO BEING AN
UNSTOPPABLE WOMAN

Erika Gilchrist

Cartoonist: D.K. Upshaw
www.ladytooner.com
219-314-3775

Thank you to my family, friends and mentors who have shown me love and support. You believed in me even when I didn't believe in myself. I love you...

And to the woman who taught me what it means to be unstoppable, I'm forever grateful for being raised by you. Thank you to my grandmother.

TABLE OF CONTENTS

INTRODUCTION

Have you ever wanted something so badly that it hurt when you didn't get it? Is there a lifestyle that you want to lead and you're not sure how to get started? I can empathize with these questions because I found myself asking them repeatedly. I kept thinking, "There **has** to be an answer. Life isn't supposed to be this difficult. What am I missing here?" When I finally found the answers, my life began to unfold in ways I had never imagined. Opportunities were revealed to me constantly, more people were willing to share their contacts and trust me with them, and I was able to get really clear about who I was and what I wanted to do. In this book I will share those secrets with you in hopes that you will soon discover how to get the things that you truly desire.

I have determined what it means for Erika to be unstoppable and my definition will not likely be identical to yours. Use these techniques as they pertain to your life; decipher the message hidden in the stories to apply them to your situation(s).

The biggest secret I learned to being unstoppable was to meditate. That may not seem like much of a secret to you, but keep reading. When you meditate (or pray, or ask a spiritual being), it's imperative that you focus on the things that you desire, as opposed to the things that trouble you. Where ever your thoughts go, so does your life. I've had women tell me, "Erika, I've tried that stuff and it doesn't work." So, I asked them to write verbatim what they were meditating about. One particular example was: *I want a life free from poverty, illness and tragedy. Keep me and my family out of harm's way, and please don't let me be misunderstood anymore at work.* Now, in reading this, you may deduce that she is meditating on having a better life. But let's look closer…

I took the piece of paper she wrote on and cut out each word individually and placed them in a box. I explained to her that the words she selected were bringing her the very things she didn't want. Her facial expression indicated she didn't understand, so I elaborated the point by asking her to draw three pieces of paper from the box. She complied and the three words she selected were "Me," "Poverty," and "Misunderstood." I explained to her that when you meditate, your focus is attracting the energy of the words you choose. So from that standpoint, she was saying she wanted poverty and misunderstanding for herself ("me"). With this in mind, let's rewrite that same meditation: "*I am living a life of abundance, health, and happiness. Thank you for the safety of my family and the clarity I provide at work.*"

If you were to put each of these words in a box, it wouldn't matter which ones you pull, because each of them attract what she actually wanted.

In writing this book, I was trying to figure out how I could drive the point 'home' on some of these topics; apply the techniques to real women so they could easily relate. Then I thought, "What better way to connect with women than to acquire real experiences from women whose stories haven't been told?" So I gathered stories that women have shared with me in past seminars and workshops, and I sought out for more true accounts that would suit the premise of this book and believe me, I received much more than I bargained for.

I have changed some of the names of these ladies to protect their privacy for reasons you will understand after reading their ordeals. I began to notice something while listening to these women; all of their stories had a very common thread. Somewhere deep within them, they knew they deserved better, but they weren't quite sure *how* to obtain better. But their 'trials-turned-triumphs,' or T3, is no different than yours. You also know that you deserve better. But the difference is that you're about to learn the *'HOW.'*

1

Ignore the Rules

As a child, I can remember many lessons my grandmother taught me. At the time, I simply did what I was told because the alternative was not pleasant. As I got older, I applied the lessons that she taught me and most of them have served me very well. Some of the most memorable were:

- If you lay down with dogs, you'll get up with fleas

- Don't seek reward for doing nice things

- When you do wrong, wrong follows you

- Treat everyone the same, regardless of race

- You don't have to *__do__* anything to someone for them not to like you

- Don't talk 'outside the house' (Keep the family's business in the family)

- A short pencil is better than a long memory

- Always be grateful for what you have

- A hard head makes a soft behind (I tested that theory on a few occasions and can certainly attest she was right)

Ignore the Rules

The most profound lesson I learned from my grandmother wasn't something she taught me deliberately. Instead, it was a subliminal message that hit me right around the age of 34 years old. I was wondering about new ventures that I could explore and how else I could enhance my life as well as the lives of others. I considered doing a book tour designed to introduce new authors to the public, I dabbled with the thought of starting a non-profit organization that would teach young girls and women how to be emotionally well, and I even mulled over starting a library that would no doubt launch a revolution of creative thinkers. And of course, I thought of writing a book that would dispel many fables young girls are taught at such a young age. (You're holding the result in your hand)

As I considered each idea, I mapped out detailed plans necessary to launch the project. I asked all the important questions like, "How much will this cost? How will this impact people? What role do I want to play? How many people will it take to have an effective team? Etc…" I would bounce around from idea to idea; each one seeming more profound than the other and I shared these ideas with a colleague of mine and she said, "Erika, you're always coming up with stuff to do. How do you know you can even do all of that?" I looked at her with a puzzled expression and that's when it hit me. It NEVER even occurred to me that I couldn't do any of them.

I was a very exploratory child; I was very curious and adventurous. I'd tell my grandmother, "I want to learn how to dance," so she enrolled me in a dance class at the local park district. I said, "I want to play the flute," so she bought me a flute and sheet music. I said, "I want to learn how to ice skate," so we went ice-skating downtown in the winter. There's a very long list of things I asked of her and not once did she say, "You can't do that." By encouraging me in my new found interests, and never telling me that I can't, I always believed *I could.* What a wonderful gift to give to a child!

But as a grown woman, I've found that going against the grain, challenging the rules, and in some cases directly defying instruction has also lead me to some desirable results and I'm happy to share those things with you here.

Use your discretion and be sure to measure all possible outcomes before proceeding to ignore rules that are set in place.

DON'T COME BACK ANOTHER TIME

One day I was in the middle of cleaning my cluttered space and the doorbell rang. It was the mail carrier and I signed for my package and collected my regular mail. Glancing through it, I noticed a flyer about a conference being held at the local learning annex. One of the speakers was Lisa Nichols, who is one of my favorite unstoppable women. Upon further inspection of the flyer, I noticed that the conference was being held that same day and I nearly dropped everything I was holding in my arms to rush to see what the current time was. I realized that I would miss the first session, but I had just enough time to get dressed and bolt out of the door and if I was lucky, I'd make it there at exactly five minutes before her last scheduled time to speak for the day. I knew that the line would likely be wrapped around the corner, but it didn't matter to me. I grabbed my camera, notebook and pen, started the car, and headed to the annex. The whole ride there I kept thinking, "No matter what, I'm going to talk to Lisa and I'm getting my picture taken with her."

I reached the parking lot and ran the entire way to the facility. It was an enormously overwhelming place that would intimidate even the most experienced traveler. I had just a few minutes before she started so I wasted no time in asking the first employee I saw where I could find the room where Lisa was speaking. He directed me across the building to the other side (of course), and off I went. Finally, I reached the door and as I suspected, there was a line containing no less than 50 people waiting to get in. As I walked closer, I noticed that the door to the conference room was closed and standing guard was a well suited tall blonde gentleman who had his arms slightly extended to his side as if to say "No one can enter." I arrived just in time to hear his announcement. "I'm sorry, but the room is at capacity and we're not admitting anyone else today. Lisa will be speaking again tomorrow at 1pm, so you can come back then. Please feel free to visit one of our other conference rooms…" He disappeared into the room and I heard the crowd groan, moan and grunt, but inevitably people began to walk away. He came back out to the hall and made the announcement again to the 20+ people who were still standing outside the door and then he disappeared into the room just as he did before. More people walked away and I stood there another 5-10 minutes or so, and there were about 8 of us left standing there still hoping to get in. The blonde haired gentleman reappeared and when he did, he looked past us down the hall, and then looked in the opposite direction as if he was looking for someone. Then, he turned his head sharply towards us and whispered, "Okay, you guys can follow me. The room is full, and there's no way I could have fit fifty more people, but I can fit eight. It's standing room only, but I can see you guys are serious about getting in so I don't think you'd care." And just like that, we got in.

Once I was inside, I scanned the crowded room for an empty seat and found one. I made my way through the crowd and asked the young lady sitting next to the empty chair if it was reserved for anyone to which she replied, "It was obviously waiting for you because for the life of me I couldn't understand why no one asked to sit here." I sat down, enjoyed the seminar and took plenty of notes. After the seminar was complete, the crowd made their way to the exit and I decided to remain in the room and wait until the pack thinned. Lisa was outside the room at a table signing autographs and taking pictures. I left the room and stood across the hall and just waited until there were just under 15 people or so standing around the table waiting to see her.

I approached the table and wiggled my way to the front and waited for the opportunity to start talking to her. I caught her eye and I said, "Hi Lisa, congratulations on your new show. I'm Erika Gilchrist and I look forward to being a guest on it." She pleasantly smiled and said, "Oh okay then girl! I'm looking forward to having you." I asked if we could take a picture together and she agreed. Whenever I look at that picture, I'm reminded of the tenacity our small group displayed in order to get what we wanted.

Rules are put in place for specific reasons, but I've come to learn that in many cases there are exceptions. Whenever possible, I seek out the exceptions to benefit my desired outcome. By doing the opposite of what we were instructed to do, we got exactly what we wanted.

"We are told never to cross a bridge until we come to it, but this world is owned by those who have crossed bridges in their imagination far ahead of the crowd."

-Anonymous

START AT THE TOP (VERSUS THE BOTTOM)

We are so often told that we need to work our way up. I have absolutely no problem with hard work and think there are no small jobs in the world. I have been everything from a housekeeper to a laborer in construction.

But I must admit I've never been one who believed in seniority for seniority's sake. The person who has been there the longest and may be the next in line, may not necessarily be the right person for the position. Instead, I'm more interested in people being matched to their passions.

Think about it. If you were hiring someone for a job, and you had two people to choose from - someone who has a lot of experience in the job you are offering but absolutely no passion for what they are doing, or someone with little experience but a lot of passion and excitement, who would you choose? I'd choose the passionate person every time because I can always train them to do exactly what I need them to do. I believe people who hire other people might have that philosophy as well. So you might as well start at the top and work your way down if needed.

Here's another way to look at it. I have a colleague named Samantha, who is a corporate recruiter for a Fortune 500 company. She told me something that I will never forget. In her career, she had posted openings for many jobs and has had thousands of people apply for her open positions. She noticed a trend among the sexes on how people apply for jobs. She said that more men than women applied for positions for which they were under-qualified. Men seemed to be more fearless in their approach for getting a job than women. Also, they were very unapologetic in their lack of experience. It was that same fearlessness that would often get them to an interview. However, she'd say the opposite with many female applicants. Women often applied for positions they were overqualified for and downplayed the experience they had. That got me thinking, "Why do you think that is?"

DON'T MIND YOUR OWN BUSINESS

Growing up, you might have heard the opposite of that a few times. I can remember many times being told to "mind your own business" when I inquired outside of the boundaries of things little children should ask about. But the importance of not minding your own business is critical to us being able to contribute our talents and

> *"The day I start minding my own business is the day my business will begin to fail."*
>
> *-Erika Gilchrist*

allow others to contribute their talents to us. It's really about the power of networking or more plainly said, the power of being nosy! Here's what I mean.

Ignore the Rules

I recently attended a pamper party for women where I was an exhibitor. The exhibit hall promised a steady stream of people I could network with to offer my services as a keynote speaker and Life Coach. I was prepared to do business; I came with hundreds of my business cards, brochures, books, CDs, and other promotional materials ready to be handed out. All I needed was for the exhibit hall to open and for me to be "On." While waiting for the exhibit hall to open, I struck up a conversation with the woman in the booth next to me. She introduced herself as D.K. Upshaw. Being my generally nosy self, I wanted to know everything...what she did, how long she had been doing it, and what kind of business she wanted from the conference. So I asked. As it turns out, she is an illustrator. It just so happens that at that very time, I was looking to hire an illustrator for my book. While we were waiting for the exhibit hall to open – waiting for what we thought was the "real business" to begin, we started our own relationship, and it was fruitful for the both of us. In fact, the illustrations found in this book are that of D.K. Upshaw.

I think that as women we have a natural knack for being a little "nosy" and as far as I'm concerned, that's a terrific trait for unstoppable women. We communicate easily - we know exactly what's going on with our girlfriends, with the neighbors, or with the other parents at school. So there is no reason not to apply this knack in other areas of your life. Talk to people, find out everything about them and look for mutually beneficial connections between you.

Secret: *Talk to people, find out everything about them, and look for mutually beneficial connections between you.*

PREPARE FOR THE BEST (NOT THE WORST)

There are plenty of good reasons to prepare for the worst – for example, you heard your mom say, "Always wear clean underwear in case you're in an accident" - but I think it's much more powerful, interesting and fun to think and prepare for the best.

I want to share a story about a colleague of mine, Sarah, who owns her own business. She's a regular churchgoer and tries her best to live by the teachings she hears on Sunday mornings. One concept that she always wrestled with was tithing. It was always her intention to tithe (give ten percent of her salary) to her church but because of the uncertainty of being in business for herself, she was always too scared to follow through. She was worried that if her business slowed or worse, failed, that she might need that money to live on and it would be gone. That's a perfect example of preparing for the worst - let me not tithe because I might not be as successful as I had hoped. She realized that that very thinking was what was keeping her small and not able to really grow her business.

So Sarah started talking to other entrepreneurs about how they got over the fear of having an uncertain income. She heard the same response from almost everyone who had achieved the level of success that she was looking to obtain. Prepare and act for the best! There was nothing wrong with her business; it was her *thinking* that was in the wrong place. She realized she needed to flip it.

So she did. She started tithing – but not just ten percent of her current salary. Sarah started tithing ten percent of her **goal** salary – the salary she had hoped to make that year. That salary was three times more than she was currently making. Something incredible happened when she did that. Not only did her thinking change, her actions changed. She stopped thinking "What will I do if I don't have the money?" to "What do I need to do to make the larger salary so I can tithe."

Even as Sarah told me her story, I could feel the intensity of her situation and I eagerly anticipated how it was going to turn out for her.

In three months time, her income had tripled. Some may call that a coincidence. Sarah doesn't. Preparing for the best has brought a whole new energy to her business because she is now *causing* her success rather than waiting for it to maybe come her way. Good for you Sarah!

> ## You know you're doing something right when you get that knot in the pit of your stomach that says you're on to something big!

IGNORING THE RULES TAKES GUTS

None of the new rules are difficult to do:

- Don't Come Back Another Time
- Start at the Top (Versus the Bottom)
- Don't Mind Your Own Business
- Prepare for the Best (Not the Worst)

But none of them is comfortable either. It's much easier to do what you've always done (or at least do what you've always been told to do.) So how do you overcome the uncertainty that comes with trying something new, especially something that's against the grain of what you've been told to do?

It's going to take you exercising a new muscle to put them in practice. It's no different than exercising at the gym. However, I'm going to suggest a different way to strengthen this "taking a risk" muscle.

When I first start working out, I'm typically very excited and try to get all the exercise that I hadn't done for the year into one day. Thus, I generally overwork my muscles. Sometimes I'm so sore the next day that I give up exercising altogether. So I'm not going to suggest taking on all four of these new rules at once. Instead, we're going to gradually strengthen our "risk" muscle through the Four Week Challenge.

For the next four weeks, you're going to focus on getting comfortable with each of the new rules. Each week, pick one of the four new rules to focus on. For example, next week select something in your life that you can focus on Preparing For the Best (instead of the worst.) Keep that one area of focus for the entire week. Hopefully in seven days you would have found at least one small success in this area. If so, select another new rule for Week Two. The idea is to start small and gain small successes. You will gradually strengthen your "risk" muscle so when you need to tackle some of the larger areas of your life, you'll be ready for the heavy lifting. Use the chart on the next page to guide you in exercising your "risk" muscle.

Week 1:

Day	Situation	Action	Result

Day	Situation	Action	Result

Day	Situation	Action	Result

Week 2:

Day	Situation	Action	Result

Day	Situation	Action	Result

Day	Situation	Action	Result

Week 3:

Day	Situation	Action	Result

Day	Situation	Action	Result

Day	Situation	Action	Result

Week 4:

Day	Situation	Action	Result

Day	Situation	Action	Result

Day	Situation	Action	Result

For those of you who work out, you understand that when you work muscles that you never use, they get sore and it can deter you from continuing the process. But unstoppable women know without a doubt that soreness is a sign of progress. Keep working that risk muscle ladies!

> "When one door of happiness closes, another opens, but often we look so long at the closed door, that we do not see the one that has been opened for us."
>
> - Helen Keller

The Secrets to Being an Unstoppable Woman

2

Get Your Butt Moving!

A dear colleague of mine once told me, "If opportunity knocks at your door, you've already missed it because your door had no business being closed." Many women sit on the inside, by the door awaiting that precious knock. And if they're preoccupied with something else, they don't get to the door in time to receive the opportunity. My advice is to keep the door open, step outside into the midst of the street, and meet & greet with opportunity. Create opportunities instead of waiting for them.

Ladies, it's time to set the record straight. Remember all those people who told you to wait for the good stuff? You know who we're talking about...the ones who tell you to wait for the right job, the right time, or the right man? Have you ever noticed how the people who tell you to wait, upon closer inspection, don't really have it all figured out? Those who tell you to stop or postpone everything until the perfect moment comes along are rarely that happy with their own life. In fact, they're likely stuck in a rut that they no longer have the ambition to get out of. The people who give the advice, telling you that you must have a solid plan before you do anything are generally repeating what they've been told. I'm here to tell you to stop waiting for the "right time!" Many women spend their entire lives waiting for the right moment to come and for many of us, it never arrives.

Get Your Butt Moving!

Now back to all that advice about slowing down…instead of slowing down or stopping all together to await that so-called perfect moment or the perfect opportunity, recognize that you have the power to create that moment to pounce. Which concept makes more sense: Waiting around for everything to be perfect, delaying the pursuit of your dreams indefinitely until you've got absolute control over your life (which may never happen anyway)…or throwing caution to the wind and taking life as it comes at you, pursuing your dreams and adapting and changing to meet the demands of the situations you find yourself in? At times, it can feel like you're in a boxing match and you can find yourself backed into a corner enduring the blows of life. But what I have discovered about unstoppable women is that, that's when they come out swinging.

Not long ago, I found myself in a situation where I felt I had nothing but undesirable options. The economy tanked, my lifestyle changed, and I was faced with possibly going back into the job market to sustain my finances. This was a very unattractive alternative because when you have an entrepreneurial spirit, you're drawn to freedom, flexibility and control, which are options you rarely get when you're working for someone else. But, in order to continue the way of life I'd worked so hard to achieve, I considered it.

In my search, I had to be very strategic. I wanted a position that paid a certain amount of money, but I didn't want a lot of responsibility because I figured I wouldn't stay very long. I found a position with a company I had worked for before because it was something I was familiar with and I knew it wouldn't take me long to be properly trained. I worked there for about a year or so when I realized that the work I was doing for them was consuming my life and not much at all was being devoted to my business. I got comfortable with the steady flow of income, the benefits, and the short commute and before I knew it, an entire year had gone by. I was feeling spiritually and creatively starved so I decided to change, yet again. But this time, I chose to do something in the field of training so I can keep my presentation skills sharp. And it was in this role that I learned to seriously move my butt.

Don't sell out your dreams for a 401K.

(Or any other monetary convenience)

THE DAY I LEARNED TO GET MY BUTT MOVING!

I was an independent contractor with a highly selective training company and I traveled across the country delivering seminars to their clients. I always assumed that the travel department has never had to travel for a living because some of the itineraries were just plain awful. They made no sense and in many cases, hours and mileage were wasted and it could have easily been avoided. But alas, I traveled like a road warrior and drudged through some undesirable weather conditions because I was doing what I loved.

I was assigned to present to an organization in Mississippi and as usual, the travel arrangements were less than pleasant. Upon arrival, my contact person was just an emotional wreck. He explained to me that he had just buried his mother the day before, he hasn't set up my classroom, and he forgot that I was even coming.

During my speaking career, I have encountered many people and their personal issues, and I've always tried to provide some sort of tangible solution they could use to better their situation. But there are some instances when you simply cannot help them; you just have to allow them to talk.

After he talked to me about his grief, he quickly added, "Oh, my goodness. I forgot to give you the check!" Generally, all payments were to be given directly to the company, not the trainer. But in his state, I gladly accepted it to send it overnight express to the company. He handed me the check and when I looked at it, it seemed like my heart stopped beating momentarily. I simply could not believe how much money the company was being paid to have me come and speak. I'm pretty quick on my feet with numbers and I quickly calculated that I was being paid *less than* 10% of the total amount. I remained calm and behaved as if everything was normal, but I could hear my heart beating loudly in my ears. Talk about putting a fire under my butt!

That day, I gave one of the most engaging presentations of my career and since then my focus has been to do seminars on my own terms. I researched how much it would cost to put all the necessary pieces into place so that I could effectively manage and maintain a successful speaking practice. That was a life-altering experience for me and I am forever grateful for it.

What's *your* defining moment? What has happened in your life that made you say, "Enough is enough. It's my turn!" If you haven't experienced it yet, ask yourself what will it take for you to get your butt in gear and make your vision manifest. Losing your job? Getting divorced? Hitting rock bottom? Getting passed over (yet again) for a well deserved promotion? Whatever your "fire" is, allow it to ignite the passion in you to begin the journey to self discovery.

BUILDING BRIDGES FROM PAIN TO PASSION

We're going to create something I call a "Success Bridge." It requires some thoughtful consideration, dedication and commitment on your part. (What, you thought this process was going to be easy?) In my short time on this planet, I've learned that if something comes to you much too easily, it's not as rewarding and it goes underappreciated. So let's build this bridge. Start by listing four of your core values. As an example, I will list mine:

1. Public Service   2. Spiritual Growth
3. Health   4. Integrity

You may very well have dozens of values, which is great, but I want you to focus on just the top four for this exercise. I've provided some examples of values from which to choose. Look through them for ideas and then list your top four (Use the blanks spaces to fill in values that may not be present):

Relationships	Family	Health	Education	Loyalty
Accomplishment	Order	Security	Faith	Religion
Challenge	Wealth	Wisdom	Pleasure	Prestige
Self Worth	Competition	Freedom	Recreation	Approval

1. _____

2. _____

3. _____

4. _____

The bridge has a series of "phases" that will get you to the other side. The first phase is your *Aspirations.* List one aspiration *per value*. For example:

PHASE ONE:
ASPIRATIONS

---

1. Help my fellow man
2. Walk in awareness & seek my 'higher self' in every situation
3. Preserve my vessel (my body) in its healthiest state
4. Keep a clear conscience and operate in truthfulness

Now, list your aspirations here:

PHASE ONE:
ASPIRATIONS

1. _____

2. _____

3. _____

4. _____

The second phase is called the ***Plan.*** In this phase, you list some actions you will take to achieve your aspirations.

PHASE TWO:
THE PLAN

1. Volunteer when I'm not asked
2. Choose to take the "high road" in difficult situations
3. Eliminate consumption of unhealthy items
4. Speak truth even when it's easier to lie

Now, list your plan of action here:

PHASE TWO:
THE PLAN

1. _____

2. _____

3. _____

4. _____

Now, we're going to **Launch** our plan, which is the third phase of the success bridge. In order to do this, we must shove our fears aside to reach the other side. In this phase, list some fears you've experienced as they relate to your plan. These fears may have kept you *from* taking action, or they motivated you to *take* them.

PHASE THREE:
THE LAUNCH

1. Being known as "Ms Goody Two Shoes"
2. Being misunderstood and alienated
3. Giving up my favorite foods and drinks
4. Not being able to sleep at night

Now, list your fears here:

PHASE THREE:
THE LAUNCH

1. _____

2. _____

3. _____

4. _____

There are action words that coincide with each list. Over the list of values, write the words **"I value."** Over phase one, write **"I will."** Over the list of phase two, write **"I will achieve this by…"** Now, write the words **"With dedication & commitment, I will eliminate my fear of…"** over phase three. Finally, at the end of the bridge, write **"Which will bring me to my…"** Here's where you tie it all together. When you string the entire bridge together, it will look like this:

I value	I will	I will achieve this by...	w/dedication & commitment I will eliminate my fear of...	which will bring me to my
	1	**2**	**3**	
	Aspirations	*Plan*	*Launch*	
_____				***Passionate Destination***
_____				
_____				
_____				

My entire "Success Bridge" statement for my <u>spiritual growth</u> value would sound like this:

"I value spiritual growth. I will walk in awareness and seek my 'higher self' in every situation. I will achieve this by choosing to take the high road in difficult situations. With dedication and commitment, I will eliminate my fear of being misunderstood and alienated which will bring me to my passionate destination."

Putting together your success bridge and referring to it regularly surely puts a fire under your butt and holds you accountable for what you say you desire out of life.

THERE'S NO SUCH THING AS RECYCLED TIME

Because time can't be recycled, you cannot afford to waste any of it. There's nothing worse than looking up one day and realizing that you could've had all the things you desired, but didn't do anything to achieve it. Barbara* can attest to this lesson all too well.

Barbara has always wanted to be a ballerina since she was a little girl. Just the thought of going to dance class would put the most glorious smile on her face. It was a constant motivator for her, even in school. She once told me that her mother said to her, "If you get good grades in school, I will sign you up for dance classes in the summer." Every year, her grades stayed above average because she was so afraid of not being able to dance. In her teenage years, she joined dance groups and performed in many different musical productions. Although it was satisfying for her to perform, she always wanted to start her own dance company.

She met a young military man who stole her heart and when he moved out of the state, so did she, just to be with him. Every place they moved to, she would research local dance companies just so she could continue to dance. Then, she had children. The dream of starting her dance company was put on hold temporarily, she said to herself. After four children, a divorce, 180 extra pounds, and being flat broke, she succumbed to the idea that it simply wasn't going to happen for her. In her late 40's she moved back to her hometown and started her life over.

Not surprisingly her youngest daughter Nina* took a liking to dance. Barbara, elated at her daughter's interest, put her in every dance class she could find. Nina started taking dance classes at age 5 and by the time she was 14, she was a flawless, technically sound ballerina. Barbara was so proud of her and one day while she was having lunch with Nina, she told her of her desires to start her own dance company. "I used to dream of having my own dance company, but those days are long gone for me," she told her young daughter. Nina asked, "Why Mommy?" Barbara told her, "Because I can't dance like I use to baby. Mommy used to be the most talented principal dancer in her troupe. But then life got in the way so it's too late for me now." Nina replied, "Mommy, you don't have to dance in order to own the company." Barbara's mouth dropped when she heard her 14 year old daughter's response. It hit her all of a sudden. Her daughter was right! You *don't* have to dance in order to run the company.

Barbara was suddenly filled with inspiration, hope, and gumption. She was so inspired to finally make her dream come true, that she researched locations, loans, and talent to get it off the ground. Fourteen months later, she opened the doors of her dance studio and she even shed 98 pounds so she could dance comfortably with her daughter. Talk about getting your butt in gear!! Up until that lunch with her daughter, she thought that her dream was dead. But why? She realized that she wasted so much time thinking about what could have been, that she missed what could be.

PERFECT SCHMERFECT!

This secret is one of the scariest things to accomplish, but it's a must do! As a business owner, I understand the importance of planning. There's no way around it in order to achieve certain goals. It has many benefits and provides an excellent blueprint. But too many women get so caught up in the planning stage, that they spend all their time planning, and no time actually doing anything. As a result, they're stuck in one place with a beautifully constructed plan without any of their desired outcomes. I'm always reminded of the mother bird who throws her chicks over the edge of the nest in order for them to learn to fly. Unstoppable women know that sometimes you have to just JUMP without your perfect plan, and figure it out along the way.

Don't expect it to be easy to say, "Dammit I'm just going to do it!" For one thing, many of the people around you, like your friends and family, may be horrified at your decision to push forward without a sound plan. Naturally, they want what's best for you, but let's face it, when it comes right down to it- it's your life right? In addition, you may find yourself disheartened when things don't go the way you want it to. Here's the big, liberating truth ladies: Most of us hardly *ever* get precisely what we set out to achieve. As time passes, our goals may change. Our circumstances may change. Our feelings may change. And during all those changes, if you're still creating the perfect plan for the original goals, you'll never catch up. If we spend our time waiting around to implement the perfect plan, we have a dangerously low chance at being unstoppable. You're left second guessing yourself; "Is *now* the right time? What about *now*? What about…"

It's particularly difficult for women to just grab life by the horns. We're expected to be the sensible ones and the voice of reason; while men are expected to be the risk-takers and go-getters. To that I say, "Oh yeah? Watch this!"

Secret: *Start implementing your plan before it's completely finished.*

Hesitation leads to devastation. Too much hesitation will cause you to miss far too many opportunities. Instead of standing there waiting for everything to be perfect, be like a tennis player…on your toes…going after every chance life serves you. Give every shot all you've got and before you know it, you'll be unstoppable.

3

Humility is Overrated

The virtue of humility certainly has its place, but when it comes to being unstoppable, you have to know when to set aside humility and plunge right into the thick of the situation. Being a life coach has many advantages. Not only do I get to assist in the navigation of another person's journey, but I learn so much from them as I'm navigating through my own. When you can absorb life lessons from coaching your clients, that's a great indicator that the relationship is truly progressing.

In this chapter, I'm going to share some common errors I've observed that women make when steering through their lives. In these cases, humility is definitely overrated.

5 DREADFUL HABITS THAT PUT THE "STOP" IN UNSTOPPABLE

If you ever wonder why things happen for other women, but it doesn't seem to happen for you, you may want to consider some simple things other women do (or don't do) to shift the course of action in your favor. In order to get what you want, you may first have to adjust some habits that are preventing you from getting ahead. At first glance they may seem baffling, but upon closer inspection you'll see how each of these awful habits stifles your eagerly awaiting unstoppableness.

1. *Over Apologizing* - Have you ever met someone whose sentences begin with "I'm sorry?" I don't mean every now and then, but nearly every time they speak, they're offering an apology for something. And many times they don't even know *why* their apologizing. It's just something they naturally say. If it's not at the beginning of the sentence, it rears its ugly head at the end.

   I worked with a young lady like this named Kim* when I was in retail management. She was a rather timid woman who wanted to please everybody and when her efforts were not satisfying to them, she dispensed several waves of apologies; so much so that they became ineffective.

   One day my district manager, Jose*, sat in on one of our staff meetings as he did several times before. When one of Kim's actions with a former customer was questioned, she didn't even offer an explanation. Instead she said, "Sorry about that." Now, I recalled the incident in question and I thought that under the circumstances, she handled the situation very well. But she couldn't find it in herself to defend her actions. So rather than divulge her thoughts to our manager, she withered and accepted the public reprimand. I then offered logical reasoning behind her actions and further explained the intensity of the occurrence. After doing so, the manager turned to her and asked, "Is that what happened?" to which she replied in a soft voice, "Yes, something like that." He snapped, "Well either that's what happened or it isn't! You can't just skirt the issue Kim; I need to know exactly what happened so I will know how to proceed, so speak up!" She simply replied, "Sorry Jose." At that point, Jose lost his temper. He glared at her and snarled, *"Would you STOP apologizing for every little thing?! Every time I turn around you're sorry about something and you know what? I'm starting to believe you!"* The room fell completely silent and all eyes were on Kim awaiting her response. What do you think the next words out of her mouth were? You guessed it... *'I'm Sorry.'* She immediately slapped her forehead as if to say 'Damn!"

I'm sure she felt embarrassed in front of her colleagues and more importantly, she felt like she let herself down. But from that point forward, there were fewer apologies uttered from her lips. I was quite proud of her in the coming months for her determination to modify that habit.

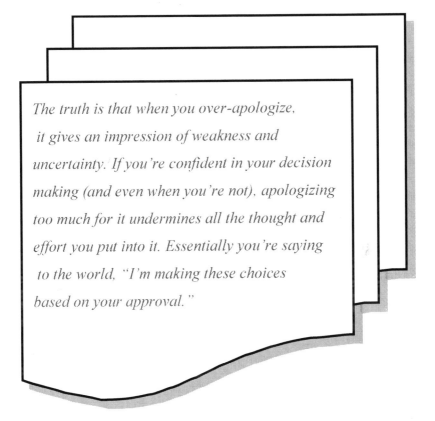

The truth is that when you over-apologize, it gives an impression of weakness and uncertainty. If you're confident in your decision making (and even when you're not), apologizing too much for it undermines all the thought and effort you put into it. Essentially you're saying to the world, "I'm making these choices based on your approval."

If there's a decision you've made and you're not 100% sure about it, simply explain the logical reasoning behind it succinctly and move on.

2. *Babbling On and On* – Surprisingly, I learned this lesson back in the seventh grade when my teacher called a classmate of mine "diarrhea mouth." Of course, at that age we all thought it was gut wrenching funny and laughed hysterically, further humiliating my classmate. But it

wasn't until my adult years that I realized the significance of what my teacher was saying. Women in general are thinkers. We think about moves we're going to make 3-4 steps ahead of time. There are so many thoughts that consume our daily lives and at times, it can be a struggle to categorize them and keep them in alignment, especially when asked a question on the spur of moment.

I remember being in a meeting when the Vice President of the company asked the room if there were any new ideas for handling a constant issue we were having amongst our employees, and Tamara* began speaking. When she opened her mouth what came out sounded something like this, "Okay, I've been thinking about this for a while and I think I may have a solution. I mean, you may not think so and that's okay, but I think it's a good idea. I even ran the idea by my husband last night after he got home from work, even though it was late because he got off an hour after he was supposed to. When I told it to him, he thought it was good, so he said I should tell you what it is. I know we have policies in place, but if we alter them I think we can resolve this reoccurring concern. Granted, it's a little unconventional but if we have an open mind I'm sure it could work, that is, unless you don't think it's a good idea..."

I will spare you the monologue that seemed to go on for five straight minutes. The VP had more patience than the rest of us because he stood there and listened to the whole spiel, nodding his head while the rest of us looked around at each other in pure frustration. After she finished, he crossed his arms and pressed his lips together as if he was attempting to hold back a boisterous laugh, cleared his throat and politely asked her, "So Tamara, what IS the idea?" It was at that moment she realized that she'd been talking but not really *saying anything*. The VP was very gracious in allowing her to continue, but I'm sure the rest of the room was thinking, "Spit it out will you?!" It didn't help her case much when she did finally reveal her idea and it wasn't very good.

One of the biggest challenges of babbling is that you disconnect with the person(s) you're addressing and your point gets lost in the shuffle. From a different perspective, when the time comes to select someone to represent a company, business, or point of view for a big deal or project, you will likely get looked over. Who wants to put a rambler in front of people who can potentially make or break their business?

3. *Being Under Prepared* – I use to look at women that seemed like they had it all and wondered, "How did they get all that? They must've had someone hand them everything. Why can't I find someone who will do that for me?" In rare cases, some women are privileged to have someone who will give them practically anything they desire. But for the rest of us, it's an on-going effort.

I was part of a women's organization and one the members, Helen*, had an excellent idea. She wanted the group to develop a strong library of resources written by members of the group so that we would have an array of books, audio, and video to assist us in our journey to success. She was a very outspoken individual, as most of us were, so she was very persuasive.

One day during a board meeting she posed the idea. She vividly described the idea and the benefits of developing the library. She even verbally illustrated what the library would look like when it's complete. Her proposal was very convincing, and the board placed it on the roster to be discussed at a later date.

She was complimented by others who were in attendance on how great the idea was and how passionately she described her vision. Not long after, the board approved the plan if she could justify expenses and time leverage. Great, right? Well…

She was elated to hear that her idea was being considered and told everyone about it in her newsletter. In the next meeting, the board was excited to hear how this plan was going to manifest. That is, until they started asking questions. According to my recollection, the conversation went something like this:

Board: *So how many books do you see in this library?*

Helen: *How many? Um… I don't know, ten?*

Board: *Ten? Just ten?*

Helen: *Uh, okay…twenty?*

Board: *Will the authors be collaborating on a single book, or will each author be responsible for a particular subject matter?*

Helen: *Well, um…a lot of ladies get along with each other so, I think we could collaborate. Or maybe not.*

Board: What topics or issues do you wish to discuss in these books?

Helen: Whatever you want I guess.

Board: What's the deadline for the first draft?

Helen: Deadline? Draft?

Board: How much will it cost the organization to launch this project?

Helen: Not too much I hope.

Board: What marketing plan do you have in mind?

Helen: Ebay.

Board: Will the authors be limited to members only, or can anyone write for the library?

Helen: Just the members, unless you think otherwise.

Board: How much will the books sell for on average?

Helen: ???????

It was just excruciating to witness. There were approximately 25-30 questions they had for her and I thought for sure the board would have stopped mid-way and reconvened when she had an opportunity to gather her facts and figures. But alas, they showed her no mercy. They adjourned the meeting very perturbed, leaving Helen humiliated and distraught.

You see, some people are the "Big Idea" people. They're very good at creating new and ingenious designs and thoughts, but they fall short in the details of the plan. It's excellent to have them on your team because they serve a great purpose, but you'll need someone like Tracey*.

Tracey was one of those people who could plan an event down to the tiniest of details. She overlooked nothing, and the elements most of us wouldn't even think of, she thought of it 5 steps ago. Tracey was in the meeting and thank goodness she took pity on Helen. Tracey assisted her in the "meat and potatoes" of the idea and resubmitted it to the board and after a few revisions to the plan, it was finally approved.

Helen was thoroughly under prepared and if it weren't for Tracey, the fantastic idea would have likely fallen by the wayside.

4. <u>*Pessimistic Thinking-*</u> We've all heard about the power of positive thought, but it's equally effective when your thought process is that of a negative nature. I keep thinking of a conference I attended and one of the speakers described how she learned how to ride a motorcycle. She said they taught her not to focus on the obstacles in the road; instead just focus on the road ahead. She said, "If you focus on the tree, you will ***hit*** the tree."

Energy is contagious whether it's positive or negative and when unconstructive thoughts emanate from you, it attracts others with the same mentality like a magnet. My grandmother once told me, "You are as good as the worst person in your circle."

5. *Giving in to F.E.A.R-* Have you ever heard of this acronym? It stands for **Forget Everything And Run!** That's exactly what fear causes us to do. We abandon all logic and reasoning and we bolt for what we think is safety and comfort. We tend to lean towards something more familiar to us as opposed to venturing out into what's unknown.

I witnessed this first hand at a temporary job I held one summer. I worked for a paper supply company and it was a relatively easy job. The general manager's name was Deidre* and the entire staff didn't like her very much. Deidre and I got along pretty well, so I didn't grasp why no one seemed to like her. She appointed another worker, Cindy* as her assistant manager. Some argued that the reason Cindy was promoted to that position was because she was the one who was the most terrified of Deidre and she could easily be controlled.

While working the front office, I recall Cindy asking Deidre how many packs of paper to order for the next month's supply. Deidre responded, "I don't know. How many packs of paper should we order for next month's supply?" Cindy shrugged her shoulders and physically shrank and said, "Well, we usually go through about four packs a month, so I was thinking maybe four." Deidre looked at her as if to say, "DUH!" and Cindy nearly burst into tears. "But what if you get mad at me if I don't order the right amount?" What Deidre said next practically blew her away. She said, "I promoted you because I thought you could handle decisions like this in my absence. I plan to move up to the Regional Manager's position and I was hoping you'd step up so I could place you as General Manager. But if you're too scared to do something as small as order paper, maybe I need to reconsider my decision."

Cindy was so fearful of Deidre's disapproval, that she couldn't make a single move without it. Cindy couldn't be trusted to run the business effectively alone because fear weighed too heavily in her decision-making.

Even if you're scared to death of what others think, it does more harm than good to allow it to hinder your creativity. When you put thought into your choices, you can better explain them. Think about how many people you've worked for who had *no idea* what they were doing. You probably wondered, "How did they get this job?" Well, for one thing, they weren't scared of making errors. And when they did, they likely brushed it off and moved on a lot quicker than someone who lived in fear.

To be truly unstoppable, you must be courageous. Doing things that don't scare you is not how courage is defined. Courage is truly defined when you're scared to death of doing something and *you do it anyway.*

BACK TO BASICS

I can recall when I was babysitting my 4 year old nephew and I was just amazed at how smart and coordinated he was. Then I asked him, "Do you know that you're the most amazing little boy in the world?" To which he replied, "Yep!" and he continued playing without stopping.

What if we had that kind of gumption? What if we KNEW that we were the most amazing beings in the world? How would our lives be different? There's a lot to learn from

> *Nobody actually wants to experience fear. We are taught to.*

children. Think of how fearless children are. They reach for things that are hot, they run out into the middle of the street without concern, and they will easily jump off of a ledge if we let them. As adults, we clearly understand why they shouldn't touch the pan on the stove, or run into traffic, or jump off the ledge, but when we correct their behavior, often times we do it in a manner that instills great fear in them; not just in that particular instance, but in other areas as well. That fear is carried within them into adulthood and they teach their kids the same thing. And the cycle continues.

YOU KNOW IT SO SHOW IT!

By definition, being humble means that a person may have accomplished a lot but doesn't feel it is necessary to advertise or brag about it. But sometimes, doing just that lands you in some very desirable positions.

I was a flight attendant for Northwest Airlines back in the late 90's and one particular week I was feeling really dispensable and uninspired. Not just in spirit, but with my appearance, my social life, and in my work. I was working with another attendant with whom I didn't seem to "connect." We weren't at each other's throats, but it was obvious we were both hoping to never work with each other again. I was at the end of a five day trip in the rear galley and I remember thinking, "Snap out of it Erika! This isn't like you. Jeez…" So I chose to have a different outlook. I went in the lavatory, where the unforgiving lights highlight every blemish, scar, pimple, wrinkle and imperfection I've ever had staring right back at me and I said, "Regardless of all that's going on it can always be worse. You're an intelligent, beautiful, and interesting person, so act like it dammit!" And just like that, I began to feel better. It was time to serve the last round of coffee to the passengers so I grabbed my full pot, my tray and cups and off I went. I felt obligated to inform my passengers that I would be coming through the aisles with scalding hot liquid so I announced in a loud voice, "Hot stuff coming through...and I've got coffee!" The passengers laughed, I laughed, and so did the other flight attendants. Remarkably, after that comment the other attendant and I got along great and we still keep in touch today.

Secret: *When you don't have any people around to support you at crucial moments, be your own cheerleader.*

PUT YOUR HAND DOWN!

As little girls, we're normally taught to speak when we're spoken to and not to talk back. There's a certain level of respect this demonstrates, but as an unstoppable woman, I say that you should speak up even if you're not being asked to talk.

One behavior that absolutely exhibits fragility is when women ask for permission to speak. At first you may think, "No way, I don't do that!" But consider this: Have you ever asked the question, "Can I say something now?" Even if it was during a casual conversation, you have literally asked for permission to speak. In the world of business, it plays a much heavier role.

Something I will never forget is when I was amidst a group of men in the break room having a heated conversation. They threw insults back and forth across the table, constantly interrupted each other, and no one wanted to back down. The only other woman in the room was Shelly* and she thought she'd take a crack at smoothing over the tension that had built up in the room. She raised her index finger, cleared her throat and said, "Excuse me, can I just say something?" No one paid her any attention, so she raised her voice, using the same gesture and repeated it. "Excuse me! Can I just say something here?" Gregory glared at her like a starving wolf and shouted, "No, you may not!" and he continued to converse with the other men. Shelly was appalled and she stormed out of the room.

My observation of those men was simple. If they wanted to say something, they just opened their mouth and said it; and it got heard! Not once did either of them ask if they could say anything. I doubt seriously if Donald Trump ever asked anyone for authorization to speak his mind. Ladies, to be unstoppable it's appropriate sometimes to put your hand down and just <u>open your mouth</u>.

THE TRUTH HAS LEGS

There's an old saying, "The truth has legs and can stand on its own." Although I learned that wise saying over a decade ago, it didn't resonate with me until years later.

I was a member of a national speaker's association and every year we had our national convention. During the convention, a representative from each local chapter would stand before the rest of the members and deliver a 5 minute speech. My local chapter held auditions to see who would represent our chapter at nationals. I was very nervous, but still confident in my ability to execute a great speech. We were given a topic by the local chairmen and each of us had approximately 5-7 minutes to deliver our talk. Some of my fellow members had been with the chapter for years and I had very recently joined so I figured I had to "wow" them in order to stand out from the others. I prepared for a week on my topic and I felt relatively comfortable with the material I created.

The day of the auditions, our names were drawn randomly to decide the order. We had to present in front of the entire chapter and the board would make the final selection. There were roughly 12 of us competing for the slot and while we were going over our notes in the wings, one of the other speakers approached me. Sheila* extended her hand and said with a suspicious smile, "I just want to say good luck to you and don't be nervous. I know you're new, and it's a lot of people watching and surely you don't want to mess up, so try to stay focused. I remember last year someone choked and everybody laughed, but I'm sure you'll do fine." She made this statement in front of everyone and when I looked around at their faces, it was as if they were eagerly anticipating my response. I've never seen a more tasteless and blatant attempt to spook another person in my life. I asked her to step outside the room so we could chat and she followed me into the hall. Once we reached a distance outside of earshot, I said to her, "You know, I teach communication skills so I'm more than familiar with various methods of manipulation. Often times, I find that when a person seeks to put someone else down, it's in an attempt to make themselves feel higher. Is that what's going on here?" She denied it as much as a person possibly could and I chose not to continue the conversation.

One by one we took our place at the podium and delivered our material to the room. When it was my turn, I stood before the room and complimented every speaker that came before me. As I delivered my speech, I could sense a shift in the room. It's something many speakers and trainers can attest to. It's when you know that the room is in sync with your message and it fuels your passion and land in a "zone" that's indescribable. I received a standing ovation at the end and the remainder of the speakers took their turns. After tallying the votes, I was awarded the spot to represent our chapter at the national convention.

I suppose Sheila figured that because I was new to the chapter, I must have been new to the world of speaking. Man, was she barking up the wrong tree! I could have easily defended my speaking ability by disclosing all of my experience and accolades, but I simply didn't feel the need. I *know* I'm a great speaker, so it was completely unnecessary to defend it. I allowed my talent to speak for itself.

See, when you know you're good at what you do, don't waste your time explaining how good you are to someone who desires to see you fold, especially when they're not even in a position to further your advancement. My truth had legs and stood on its own and so does yours, so show em' the way ladies!

Secret: *Demonstrate great leadership by saying, "Let's go!" instead of dictatorship and saying, "Go!"*

4

Five Things Unstoppable Women Do

As a life coach, I'm constantly faced with researching how to assist others in resolving or better managing their issues. This requires a wide array of resources to do the job successfully. What I've found is that each woman I coach seems to think that their situation is unlike any other. Sometimes I hear, "Erika, get ready for this one, because it's going to blow you away!" And sometimes their stories are intriguing, but not uncommon. There's a common thread of deception, poor judgment, lack of effort, and unforeseen events that tie these experiences together.

What I decided to do was put together the top five trends I've observed from those women who seem to ask for (and get) what they want. There were many traits from which to choose and my biggest challenge was deciding which ones to isolate into a single chapter. I have selected these five because if you start here, the rest of the journey becomes a little less frightful. In my research, I've interviewed mentors, business owners, and other successful women about how they get to (and remain) at the top of their game. The most common action these unstoppable women do is call upon someone they trust to aid in the progression of their goals.

1. BUILD A STRONG POWER CIRCLE

What is a "Power Circle?" A power circle is a group of people you surround yourself with who helps you to grow, improve and evolve. Because all people don't have the same strengths and weaknesses, each person in your circle is going to serve a different purpose. You call upon them as necessary to meet your specific need(s).

It's helpful to have a *visual* power circle to place on your refrigerator, in your office, at your desk, or on your desktop to keep you grounded. Start by drawing a large circle with a smaller circle within it. Then, draw straight lines from the outer edge of the smaller circle to the edge of the larger circle creating different sections. The number of sections depends on how many people are in your circle. Next, place each person's name within a section in any order that you wish.

After you've done this, consider what each person has to offer. Think of a strength associated with that person and place that strength on the outside of the circle next to their name. Think of the people you have in your life. Which one gives you tough love, sensitivity, insight or some other advantageous quality? If you're a relatively meek woman and you find yourself in a situation that requires a strong personality, who would you choose to come to your defense? It's good to have various personalities within your circle. You would have a pretty dull and boring existence if all the people in your circle were exactly like you. You need to have a well "seasoned" sphere in order to take full advantage of what it has to offer your world. So what does a power circle look like? An example of how it will look is provided on the following page.

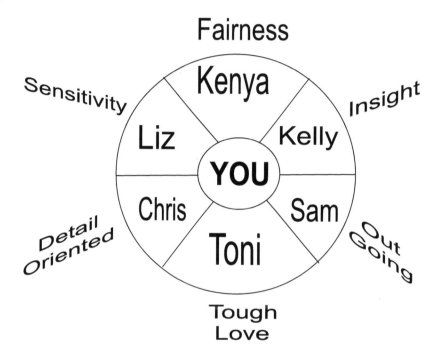

The Power Circle ™

Fairness

Sensitivity

Insight

Kenya

Liz · YOU · Kelly

Chris · Toni · Sam

Detail Oriented

Out Going

Tough Love

Here's how it works. If you are in a position where you know you were at fault, but you've learned your lesson and you just need to talk, you can look at your power circle and probably choose to talk to Liz because of her <u>sensitivity</u>. If there's something you really want to achieve, but you haven't taken steps toward attaining your goal, Toni will be the one to give you the kick in the pants you need to get moving because she demonstrates <u>tough</u> <u>love</u>.

I can recall running into an old high school friend of mine in a mall last year. She and I spoke briefly and when I asked her about her life, I began to remember why she and I never stayed in touch. Her conversation consisted of nothing but put-downs and sarcasm of other people and she'd always been that way. She asked if we could go out sometime and play catch-up with our lives, hanging out like we did back in high school. One part of me was saying, "Erika you have to be more sympathetic. After all, she has been your friend for the last 15 years." So I gave her my number so we could talk soon. Days later, I was explaining to a current friend of mine about some of my experiences with my old buddy in the past, and my friend said something to me that hit me as hard as bricks. She said, "Erika, don't feel obligated to keep her in your life. She hasn't been your friend for the last 15 years; instead, she was your friend *15 years ago*."

See how having a power circle can help keep things in perspective? Use your power circle to assist you in being unstoppable. Below you will see an empty power circle. You may copy and enlarge it to create your own front-line.

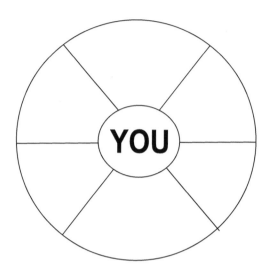

If you allow it, your visual power circle will serve as a constant reminder that you are not alone in your journey to being unstoppable. You may add or delete as many names as necessary to complete it. Please note that your power circle will likely change as time progresses. You may also note that there may be names that remain in your circle for as long as you have it. Oppositely, there may be names that change as you deal with varying problems in your life.

Power circles can also be separated into various areas of your life. For example, you may have power circle for your place of work, one for your family issues, and another for social surroundings.

2. SAY 'NO'

This is one that many women struggle with. There are many reasons women have a difficult time saying no to people:

- Feeling Guilty
- Fear of retaliation
- Hurting someone's feelings
- Maybe they won't like you

and many other reasons…

But unstoppable women understand that saying 'no' is a very important step in achieving and maintaining self esteem and to reduce the damage caused by bad stress. But *how* do you actually say it? What words or phrases do you say to tell someone you're turning down their request and still sound assertive even though you're terrified?

Use the **E.G.O. Method ™**

E *XPRESS UNDERSTANDING*
G *IVE THE SITUATION*
O *FFER AN ALTERNATIVE*

When saying no, try not to use these words: **No, can't, but, however, unable to, and unfortunately.** When people hear these words, they know that their request is about to be turned down. Once they realize that, unpleasant attitudes and resistance start to emerge and now you'll have a whole new set of issues to deal with.

How would you handle this common scenario?

It's ten minutes before Sarah is scheduled to leave work. Her boss asks her to stay late to help the team meet a project deadline. Sarah has a child in daycare that she must pick up within the hour so she's not able to stay late.

The conversation can go in many different directions, depending on the personalities involved, but typically the conversation will go something like this:

Mr. Smith: *Sarah, we fell behind on this project and I need you to stay late to help the team catch up, okay?*

Sarah: *Uh, I'm sorry I can't because I do have to pick up my daughter from daycare so I'm unable to stay late today.*

Mr. Smith: *Can't you find someone else to pick her up? This project is for our biggest client and I really need you to be a team player.*

Sarah: *(Reluctantly) Okay, I'll see what I can do.*

Mr. Smith: *Good, I expect to see you in the conference room in twenty minutes.*

Unfortunately, this will create more undesirable predicaments in both Sarah's personal and professional life. At this point, Sarah has to call upon someone in her family or friends to drop what they're doing to not only pick up her child, but to baby sit for an undetermined amount of time.

Let's try Sarah's response again, this time using the E.G.O. Method.

> **Express Understanding**- *"Mr. Smith, I understand that this project is very important to the company, if it wasn't you wouldn't be at my desk right now.*
>
> **Give Situation**- *My situation is that I have to pick up my child from daycare and there's no one else available to do it.*
>
> **Offer an Alternative**- *I will come in early on tomorrow, work through lunch, and help the team catch up as much as we possibly can."*

Sarah just told her boss 'no' without using any of the above mentioned trigger words. In a perfect world, there will always be an alternative to offer. But as you are well aware, sometimes you have no other options. In the above scenario, what if the deadline was *today*? You can't offer to come in on tomorrow because it's not an option. If that was the case, Sarah would then say:

Express Understanding- *"Mr. Smith, I understand that this project is very important to the company, if it wasn't you wouldn't be at my desk right now.*

Give Situation- *My situation is that I have to pick up my child from daycare and there's no one else available to do it. Perhaps with some prior notice I could have made some arrangements. At this point, it's too late in the day."*

After that statement, it's important to *stop talking.* Allow the other person to speak so you'll have an idea of where they are with your answer. Some people will go so far as to threaten you without even realizing they've done it. What if Sarah's boss responded with, "I thought I could really count on you Sarah, but I clearly see that you're not a team player. Frankly, I'm surprised at your reluctance especially with your evaluation fast approaching." Do you see the underlying threat?

At this point, many women would cave in and say yes out of fear of losing their job. But unstoppable women understand that their talents have been called upon for a reason and therefore they have leverage. An unstoppable woman's response may be, *"Mr. Smith, what I hear you saying is that I have to choose between my job and my child. Is that what you're asking me to do?"* Legally, he cannot say yes without risking a lawsuit.

> # Unstoppable women know that no one else will value your time until YOU do.

WHAT ARE YOU SAYING 'YES' TO?

When you say 'no' to one thing, you're saying 'yes' to something else. When Sarah told her boss that she wasn't going to stay late, she was saying 'yes' to the value she placed on her time.

> ### When you say "No"...
> *"This behavior is unacceptable to me."*

> ### You're Saying "Yes"...
> *"I have self respect and I will not be treated like anything less than dignified."*

> ### When you say "No" to:
> *Sitting down for other people...*

You're Saying "Yes" to:
Standing up for yourself!

3. CLEAN HOUSE

Unstoppable women get rid of those people in their lives who attempt to stifle their growth. These are the people who have no desire to see you get ahead. They may constantly splash pessimistic remarks your way every time you speak of something positive you want to do. I call them "Break-Down Specialists." Anything they *can* do to contribute to the demise of your prosperity and happiness they *will* do. Whether you create distance or eliminate them all together, you must first recognize who these people are.

First, take inventory of the people in your life. Using the chart below, assess how you truly view your current relationships. Place a check mark in all boxes that apply.

	Spouse/ Partner	Parents	Children	Siblings	Friends	Co-Workers	Other
I'd like to spend more time with…							
This relationship drains me…							
I should spend more time with…							
I wish I didn't have to spend as much time with…							
I really enjoy this relationship…							
I spend the right amount of time with them…							

You now have evidence of what you've known all along. You know where you're spending too much of your time, where you should spend more of your time, and where you'd like to spend more of your time. Armed with this information, you can now begin the elimination process. It's important for you to know that some of the people you remove may be related to you or have been in your life for many years. This can be especially difficult, but it's necessary to create a strong power circle.

4. DON'T PLAY VICTIM

Unstoppable women know that the role of 'victim' does not set well to achieve desired results. When you're constantly blaming others for your circumstances and conditions, you have taken on that detrimental role. Ironically, many women don't even realize they have undertaken that position and to tell them that they have can be disastrous. Perhaps you know someone who blames all their problems on someone else, or no matter what happens, they claim it's not their fault. Now ask yourself, is that person *you?* So how can you tell if you're playing the role of victim? A clear indication lies in the type of questions one asks themselves when faced with a dilemma.

The type of questions fall in one of two categories: *Victimization or Ownership.* On the following page you will see specific questions commonly asked and the category under which they fall.

Victimization	**Ownership**
1. Why are they doing this to me?	*1. Why am I allowing them to do this to me?*
2. How can I change them?	*2. How can I change my response to their actions?*
3. Why me?	*3. Why NOT me?*
4. Why can't they just understand me?	*4. How can I communicate with them more effectively?*

After reviewing these questions, ask yourself which role you play. If you're not satisfied with the answer, you can make the choice to change it at any time. Why? Because that's what unstoppable women do!

5. Pinpoint the Source of Conflicts

Have you ever had an argument or disagreement with someone and had no idea what was really going on? What about the time you and your co-worker didn't see eye to eye on a project and you simply could not understand why they couldn't see your reasoning? I'm about to show you the source(s) of 98% of all conflict.

1. PRECEDENCE	*Each person believes their position is more important than the other's.*

	Example: Diane can't complete her portion of a project until her co-worker provides her with some information. Her co-worker Kyle wants to take his time and research the information to ensure its accuracy even if it means coming really close to the deadline.
2. LACK OF INFORMATION	*Someone does not have all the correct information and is acting based upon what they believe to be true.* ***Example:*** *Tina is upset with her boss because she was not awarded any vacation days at the end of the year. Her boss informed her that she wasn't eligible until her 1 year anniversary with the company.*
3. DESIRED OUTCOMES	*This is when you don't have the same goals.*

	Example: Valerie and her mother are arguing all the time because Valerie wants to marry her current boyfriend and her mother thinks he's a loser.
4. GOVERNING VALUES	*This can be how you were raised, the different cultural environments you're accustomed to, or your current belief system(s).* *Example: Gary and Samantha have a child and Gary wants to take the child trick-or-treating for Halloween. Samantha refuses to allow the child to participate in the holiday because she believes it's wrong.*
5. THE PROCESS	*This is when you cannot agree on **how** the process should go.* *Example: Hannah and Mike work together and they have to file client folders. Hannah*

	wants to file them alphabetically and Mike wants to file them by according to their client numbers.
6. DELIVERY OF MESSAGE	*Simply put, this is the **way** they convey the message to you.*

Secret: *Pinpoint the root of the problem(s) so you'll know where to start the resolution or management of the conflict.*

Apply these five things to your life and you will surely be on your unstoppable way!

5

Get Beside Yourself

You probably have heard it said that, "When Mom's not happy, no one's happy!" So you always need to take care of Mom. That's the essence of "Get Beside Yourself." As women, we are often so quick to be there for everyone else, we generally put ourselves last. This wouldn't really be a huge problem if in most cases, we actually got around to taking care of our own needs. But too often, there's always just one more person to take care of, and our needs, hopes and dreams get put off for one more day, never coming to fruition.

It starts with something as simple as that unread book that lays beside you on the nightstand because you're too exhausted at the end of the day to enjoy that small pleasure. But it also includes larger endeavors, such as never turning your lifelong dream into that business you've always wanted. Or, it can even become life threatening when we begin to neglect our well-being or take on unhealthy behaviors.

It's not just in taking on new projects where we need to get beside ourselves. It's also in our relationships with other people. You might have a relationship or two…where to be content, you might need to release and let go of something…or maybe even release and let go of someone. Sometimes we are so preoccupied with taking care of the other person's needs that we don't even consider, much less ask for, what would make us happy.

I learned this from my childhood friend's grandmother, Ms. Haddie*. I always looked forward to going to my friend's house because Ms. Haddie always had a funny story, or some good food that she eagerly shared with me. As I grew older, I became more observant of her lifestyle. One day, I had a long talk with her and her story amazed me.

Raising children was something that she had always looked forward to in her life. She was blessed to have three children of her own. However, due to some unforeseen events that sometimes happen in families, she ended up raising her children and some of her grandchildren - a total of nine children in all.

I don't think it was ever part of her plan to raise six additional kids, but as women often do, we step in whenever necessary (not just when it's convenient.) And Ms. Haddie did it cheerfully, knowing that the job had to be done. But what happened in the process is that the hopes and dreams that she had for herself were put on hold.

See, Ms. Haddie always dreamed of becoming a fashion designer. Her plans were to attend a school for Fashion Design and one day design high-end clothes for A-list stars. But those plans were temporarily put on hold once she had children. The plan was to stay home to take care of her children while they were young and then once they were all in school, she would go to school to pursue her dream.

She continued to hone her natural talent for designing clothes while her children were young. When anyone in the neighborhood needed a prom or wedding dress, it was always Ms. Haddie they sought out. Whether it was a dress that needed to be altered or a suit that need to be tailored, it was she who would do the job. She continued to work with fashion to keep her dream alive that one day she would get to focus on her own needs and get a degree in fashion.

As her third child was going off to school, she began to get things in order to apply to school. But when a family member got caught up with drugs and was unable to care for her own child, it was she who took in the child as if she was her own. That was child number four and the start of a new trend. Before she knew it, there were other family members who experienced similar problems or situations of young parenthood and unhealthy lifestyles that led to numbers five, six and seven. Before you know it, Ms. Haddie was up to her ninth child and the dreams of a career in fashion were permanently put on hold.

If you ask her, she had no regrets in taking on the raising of all nine children. Although hard work, it is one of the shining achievements in her life. But ever so often, as she's watching the red carpet of the Oscars or checking out Oprah's latest outfit, I'll hear her say, "I could have designed that." She begins to think about what could have been.

So it was at age 65 when she was asked to raise baby number ten, that she stopped and said, "No more! I'm done raising babies. It's time for me to do for me." From that point forward, things changed.

- She started to travel – destinations like Mardi Gras, Hawaii and the Bahamas – and all flying first class.

- Several years after her husband passed, she started to date again – her new boyfriend twenty years her junior. (Who knew Ms. Haddie was a cougar!)

- And she's even taken a few classes (Who knows?...a school for Fashion Design may still be in her future.)

When I asked her what the biggest change has been she said, "I now wake up when my body is through sleeping!" That's a far cry from getting up when one child is crying or when another needs to go to their dance class early on a Saturday morning. In turn, I've noticed that once she "got beside herself," she became more alive, more open and more available to all of us that she so dutifully took care of for so long.

When I'm running myself ragged, trying to take care of everyone else around me, I try to remember that the best way to give of myself is to get beside myself, because it is only then that I can be truly available to those I'm trying to support.

> ## "No bird soars too high if he soars with his own wings."
> ## *- William Blake*

YOU'VE GOT THE GOODS!

In the world of business, I've seen the consequences of not getting beside yourself happen too many times with some of my friends and colleagues. Crystal* is a good example.

Crystal had always dreamed of publishing her own magazine that would focus on health and fitness. From a distance, it seemed she had everything it took to do it.

- She was smart – she graduated with a degree from an Ivy League university.

- She had experience – she had worked as an editor for various health and fitness focused magazines for over 15 years.

- She was good at what she did – she was well-respected by her peers in the industry.

But one thing she was not good at (or at least she believed she was not good at) was "selling herself."   To make it in publishing, you have to have advertisers. Your job is to essentially convince advertisers to believe that people will buy your magazine and thus see their products. Even though Crystal had a very outgoing personality, she never felt confident in selling her ideas and was afraid she would not be taken seriously. So her dreams of starting her own publication were infinitely on the back burner for the "one day" that had never come.

A good friend of ours named Simon* was starting his own fitness magazine, and he offered her a job as Head Editor. He knew that she had what it took to turn out a great magazine so he felt very confident leaving the bones of the business to her, while he concentrated on securing the advertising needed to fund it.

In the first year, the magazine only had enough advertising to be printed four times. Not bad for a start-up. But Simon wanted to make it a monthly publication and needed to raise advertising sales to do so. So when Simon started meeting with advertisers who wanted to know more about the magazine, he would bring Crystal along to the pitch meeting. What Crystal didn't realize was that she was completely compelling in selling her ideas for the magazine because she was so passionate about health and fitness. When Crystal was present in the meetings, she always sealed the deal.

Over time, many of these same advertisers began to realize that the person who knew the most about the magazine was Crystal and they began to contact her directly, instead of Simon. As you probably can guess, this angered Simon. Crystal did her best to redirect the advertisers back to Simon as she wanted to "stay in her lane" and do what she was hired to do, but they continued to contact her and wanted her present at the meetings. Simon's resentment continued to build toward Crystal. After a disagreement one day about a minor issue in the layout of the magazine, Simon fired Crystal.

Crystal was crushed. She had never been fired from a job before. The firing had taken her by surprise, especially since she had been doing a great job in her position. But she knew that

Simon couldn't bare some of the attention that the advertisers had shown her. She was saddened by the experience because all she had ever wanted to do was to help make the magazine a success for her friend.

Her first reaction was to be depressed about the experience. After a few months had passed by, the depression turned to anger. She kept asking herself, "Why exactly did he fire me?" She knew that she had begun to be too successful in the advertising meetings. But then it really hit her. She was **successful** in the advertising meetings! Wasn't it the fear of "selling" her ideas the only reason she had not started her own magazine? The irony of the situation had finally hit her. Well if she was good enough to raise advertising dollars for Simon's magazine she must be good enough to do it for herself. Two years later, Crystal launched her first issue of her own health and fitness magazine.

That's the perfect example of getting beside yourself. See, Simon knew Crystal's potential. The advertisers knew her potential. But no one was going to make it happen for her - ride in and be her knight in shining armor. She had to become her own best ally and do it for herself. She had to deal with the fears that she had about herself and her own capabilities, because those fears were the only things holding her back.

See, no one's going to tell you that you have the skills, the intelligence or the gumption to make it happen for you – whatever "it" is. You've got to be your own best cheerleader and figure out what's standing in the way of what you want. Because in the end, you'll either have what you want or you'll have all the reasons why you <u>don't</u> have what you want. Which would you rather have?

But you might ask yourself, if you're always the one who helps everyone else get what they want, how do you find the support you need to make your dreams happen? In essence…who motivates the motivator?

Well, how do world class athletes move themselves to the next level to achieve extraordinary results? They hire a coach!

SOUND THE WHISTLE!

Let's first talk about what a coach is. Coaching is often confused with therapy so let's discuss the differences. Now these differences have been examined and explained by PhDs, so I will not attempt to make distinctions at that level. I'll just highlight some general differences between them.

Therapy helps you examine your past to make sense of the actions you are taking in the present. In therapy, you will also examine your emotions and how they are a driving force in your actions. Coaching is focused on the future that you want to create and the actions that you will need to take in the present to make that future a reality. For example, let's say you have a communication issue with a significant other. In therapy, you might examine other people in your past you have had a similar communication issue with to shed light on why you are having the issue. In coaching, you focus on what actions need to be taken to resolve the communication issue and your emotions are more of a bystander to the process. Both can be very effective in bringing about behavior change. Here's a visual example of the difference:

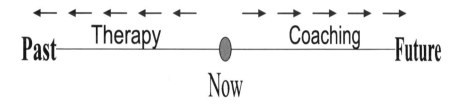

So why hire a coach instead of a therapist? Let's go back to the world-class athletes. Every serious athlete has a coach as an outside observer of their actions. If the athlete is not following through when shooting the ball or consistently hitting the net on their tennis swing, the coach, as an expert observer, recognizes the shortcoming and works with the athlete to correct it. The coach doesn't have to have achieved the level of excellence as the athlete, but they at least have to be proficient. Phil Jackson, Coach of the Chicago Bulls from 1989-1998, was no Michael Jordan, but he knew how to play basketball well. What he really knew how to do though, was motivate Michael Jordan to improve upon his talent to be the best basketball player we have ever seen.

So why do you need a coach? For some reason, we seem to be more accountable to others than we are to ourselves. (I seem to cheat less when I'm dieting with friends than when I'm trying to lose weight on my own.) A coach gives us a structure to be accountable to someone else who has our desired result as their goal. Let's go back to my friend Crystal who hired a coach as she was starting her business.

Even though Crystal had gained confidence in the area of selling her ideas to prospective advertisers, she knew herself well enough that when the road began to get rough, she might back down. So she hired a coach. She met with her coach weekly to discuss the actions she was taking to start her business. She made weekly promises as to what she would do from one week to the next. In the event she didn't achieve her goal, she would review what may have prevented her from taking the actions she needed to take. She told me that she would often hear her coach's voice in her head as she was getting ready to take the actions she had promised, and often times that voice was the only reason she would keep her promise.

In the event she did not keep her promise, they would have a conversation to discover what had taken her off track. In most cases, it simply came down to fear. (How many times have you let fear derail you from getting what you want? It usually is at the center of it all.) Having a coach gave her a place to acknowledge where she had let fear stop her in her pursuit, acknowledge it, and make a new promise to get back on track.

What I found most interesting is that she and her coach didn't always talk about her business. Sometimes it was something that was going on in other aspects of her life was taking her off track in her business. Once she explained that she was having trouble with having advertisers call her back. It seemed that everyone had stopped communicating with her. After a conversation with her coach, she realized that she had been fighting with her husband and had been giving him the silent treatment. Her coach's instruction was to work out the disagreement with her husband. She did and mysteriously the phones starting ringing again at work. It turns out that our lives aren't as compartmentalized as we'd like to think.

Now you might be wondering, "Do I have to pay for a coach?" "Can't I just find a friend who can hold me accountable?" My answer to the second question is that it's possible but difficult for someone to champion your cause without letting their idea of who you are stand in the way. Also, when we pay for services, we take them more seriously. We don't place as much value and seriousness on things we get for free.

So here's your assignment for how to "get beside yourself." Hire a coach. You might now be thinking, "How do I hire the right coach?" Interview coaches to find the right person - someone you vibe with and you feel is connected to you and your vision for yourself. In fact, here are five questions you'll want to ask:

1. What type of coaching do you specialize in?

2. Do you have any testimonials from previous clients?

3. Where did you receive your training?

4. What are your ethics codes?

5. Will this be one-on-one or group coaching?

And coaching is not just for starting a business. There are Life Coaches, Spiritual Coaches and Health and Fitness Coaches – each having their own area of expertise.

The one common denominator is that the right coach is someone you will be able to count on to champion what's important to you, even when you may not be able to take that stand for yourself!

Although this phrase gets negative reviews, I'm putting a positive spin on it. When I say 'get beside yourself' I mean *be your best ally*. Stand by your own side because I'm sure you realize that not everyone has your best interest at heart. In looking around for someone to help you in what seemed to be a crisis situation, you may have heard things like, "I wish I could help but…, I don't know let me get back to you…" Then there's the infamous scenario when no one returns your calls when they find out you need help. Well ladies, it looks like it's up to you to be there <u>for you.</u>

GET TO KNOW YOURSELF

Self awareness is essential in being unstoppable. Get to know why you react the way you do. How your thoughts affect how you feel, how your feelings affect your choices, and how your choices affect the outcome of the situation. Look at the chart and let's examine this cycle more closely.

YOU: This represents all of your experiences, past and present. Everything that you have come to know is in the midst of everything.

Thinking: What has happened to you in the past affects what flows into your thoughts. For example, if you're introduced to the possibility of a new romantic relationship, the thoughts of past relationships may immediately flow through your mind. You think of the roller coasters, the let-downs, how you tried to make it work and how it seemed to crumble right before your eyes.

Now these thoughts flow right into your emotions...

Feelings: All the hurt, frustration, and anxiety that you once felt emerge to the surface. You begin to experience the actual emotions associated with that previous relationship. You may even cry when you're alone or lash out at someone when you're angry because the emotions are so raw.

Now these feelings affect our decision making...

Choices: You may choose to disregard the possibility of a new relationship because you don't want to go through a similar situation. Or you may make choices that reflect the previous relationship. For example, you may be suspicious of your new found friend because your previous companion cheated. You may call too frequently just to see what they're doing, or accuse them of sleeping around with their friends. You do this so you don't feel like a fool ever again.

Ah, the results of our choices...

Outcome: Your relationship is full of tension and the trust is damaged even before it had an opportunity to grow. Your companion doesn't feel comfortable sharing things with you out of fear that you will turn it into something "wrong" and it eventually leads to the demise of the relationship.

But here is where it gets interesting...

You say to yourself, "Humph! I didn't think it was going to work anyway." Did you notice the word *think* in that sentence? The cycle has started all over again! Be aware of *what* your thinking, *why* you're thinking it, and the possible outcomes of allowing those thoughts to enter your mind.

TALK TO YOURSELF

No worries ladies, you're not mentally unstable for doing this, so relax. I'll share something with you, all of the unstoppable women I know admit to talking to themselves quite often. Sometimes it's a quick pep talk, and other times it's a longer, deeper conversation.

You can start by talking yourself *out* of those unconstructive thoughts. So how do you do that? Let's start by filling in the blanks below.

"I'm thinking these thoughts because _____..."
"Are these thoughts based on the current situation, or am I rehashing a previous experience?" _____
"Some possible results of these thoughts are _____..."

A close associate of mine once shared that she was overwhelmed with anxiety about a job she was applying for with a prestigious company. While she was sitting in her car in front of the office building minutes before the job interview, she noticed that she began to think about a previous promotion that had come available and how she was sure she'd get it. It was given to someone else and she was furious. All of the betrayal and anxiety that consumed her then began to consume her at that moment. That's the experience that prompted her to seek employment elsewhere. Then she began to wonder what would happen if she didn't get this job. She'd have to stay at that dreadful place longer than she wanted, and she wouldn't be able to move out of her tiny apartment into a house because of her lack of finances. Then she began saying to herself, "Fiona*, you have the experience, education and passion that's needed to do well in this position. They'd be foolish not to hire you. I know you're nervous and it's natural, but you're nervous for the right reasons. That other job wasn't for you, otherwise you'd have it. _This_ job is yours, so claim it!" The result? Not only did they hire her, but they offered her a position higher than the one for which she applied. It helped that she was well qualified, but she wasn't afraid to talk to herself and eliminate those negative thoughts when it was crucial to do so. She talked herself "off the ledge" and it worked out well.

Give yourself a good talking to when it's necessary. And not just when you need a pep talk, but when you make an error give yourself permission to let it go. You can say, *"Self, you made a mistake which doesn't make you inferior, it's makes you human. It even makes you smarter. Let's not make choices that will land you in this position again and get past it. **I am okay.**"*

6

Side with the Enemy

The moment I thought of this chapter title, I knew eyebrows would raise and mouths would curl wondering, "What are you talking about Erika?" I mean part of being unstoppable is to learn how to deal with your enemies right? So why would I want to be on their side?

Remember, we're talking about revealing the secrets to being unstoppable, and this one is huge...ready? JUST BECAUSE THEY VIEW YOU AS THEIR ENEMY, DOESN'T MEAN YOU SHOULD VIEW THEM AS YOURS.

This particular secret is something I learned in the midst of a heated discussion I was having with a young woman who called my phone late one night. Allow me to explain...

Some years ago, I met a man with whom I had started dating. We went out probably two or three times and I thought he was a nice person. He didn't appear very secretive, and he was forthcoming with answers when I asked them. He had five children, never married, currently single, and working at the same place for over 15 years. I had visited him at his home and noticed it was a typical 'bachelor' pad. He had no furniture, the fridge was packed with beer and leftovers and none of his towels matched. Still, he was very respectful and kind to me, so none of that really mattered. I figured if anything, I made a new friend.

About a month had gone by and late one night my cell phone rang. I looked at the caller ID and it was an "Unknown" caller. I didn't answer. It rang again, and I figured it could be an emergency, so I picked up. The voice on the other end said, "May I speak to Erika?" I revealed myself and her conversation went something like this:

(In a loud furious tone) "Erika my name is Rita* and I want to know what you're doing with my man! He may not be perfect but he's mine. We've been together for 6 years and we have children together so whatever you two got going on it's about to cease..." She continued on for what seemed to be 4-5 minutes and I never said a word. It seemed as though she realized she'd been the only one talking because she abruptly said, "HELLO?!" Here's how I responded in a calm, low voice:

"Excuse me, what did you say your name was? Rita I completely understand why you called me. If I were in your position, I'd be calling the other woman too. I didn't know anything about you and if I had, I would have walked away. I don't wreck homes and I respect people's boundaries. I remember when I found out that my ex had another girlfriend and I found myself calling the other woman as well so I've been where you are and I know it doesn't feel good. In fact it really sucks. I'm so sorry you're going through this. How many kids do you have?"

She proceeded to tell me about her family in a much calmer tone and she began to cry. She explained that she's had to go through this several other times during the course of their relationship. I told her that she deserves better and asked her why she decided to stay. "Because of the kids," she replied. We stayed on the phone for about 45 minutes and she became one of my coaching clients.

Secret: *Don't match negative energy when you want to be heard.*

TELL THEIR STORY

In moments of heated debate, the goal of most people is to get their point across. It matters very little what you have to say if they haven't conveyed their point to you to their satisfaction. When they don't think you "get it," they're likely going to talk and talk until they believe you do. There's a shortcut through all of that dialogue and when I practice this technique, it casts a blanket of composure over the conversation.

You're going to state the situation from their point of view. For example, Jamie and Fatima are engrossed in an argument. Jamie has been staying late at work because her relief, Fatima, has been arriving to work late. Jamie isn't allowed to leave her post until Fatima shows up. The ladies get along relatively well, but this situation is creating tension. Fatima has been told on two occasions that her tardiness is a problem and this particular day, she was running late again. (Side note: Fatima has been making flimsy excuses in an attempt to cover the real reason she's been late. She got evicted from her apartment that was conveniently located by the train, and now she has to rely on others to transport her to and from work because she can't afford a cab, and she's embarrassed about it.) Fatima genuinely felt awful about being late and she knew she couldn't hide her situation much longer. When she walked into work, late again, Jamie began to express her disgust.

As the conversation began, Fatima knew what direction it was going in and when she saw Jamie building a temper, she said this, "*Jamie, you have every right to be upset. You show up on time to relieve your co-workers and you deserve the same respect. When you get off work late, you're forced to pick up your children late from school. Your ride has to wait outside longer than necessary and it's not fair to them. You've talked to me on numerous occasions, and I appreciate you trying to settle this between us first as opposed to going to management.*" Jamie's demeanor began to relax slightly as Fatima continued, "*If I were in your position, I would feel taken advantage of and dismissed. It*

111

isn't my intention to do any of that and I'm truly sorry. Please forgive me." Fatima took a deep breath and revealed the true reason she has been late and to her surprise, Jamie was very sympathetic to her situation. Jamie had been evicted before and shared that information with Fatima. They worked out a plan that worked for both of them.

If Fatima hadn't started with the challenges that Jamie faced, the conversation could have potentially escalated to an undesirable place. Be mindful that this technique won't likely work when you're insensitive or just trying to get the other person to shut up. What comes from the heart, touches the heart, so be sincere.

SAY WHAT?

The primary cause of misunderstandings is when someone doesn't actually listen to the message being conveyed by the other person. In other words, 'half-listening.' Here's what happens during most arguments: Jackie* and Elaine* are having a heated discussion and their points are in direct opposition. Their voices start to escalate, their body language becomes more aggressive, and eventually name-calling and insults can be slung back and forth. Even if they pretend they're listening, it's not likely you're being heard when they have more to say.

Consider this: when you're engaged in an argument, and the other person is either shouting or speaking in an angry tone, you're usually focusing on what you're going to say next. And you're just waiting for them to pause long enough for you to spew your thoughts. When you find a break, you start speaking your mind, thinking that you're really getting across to them. After all, you've given this a lot of thought right? But guess what they're doing while you're talking? They're thinking about what they're going to say when *you* take a pause. With both of you concentrating on your next reply, nobody has heard *anything*.

<u>Secret</u>: *When you're engaged in conversation, instead of 'half-listening,' jot down a word or short phrase to remind you of the point you wanted to make. If you're not in a position to write anything down, make a few mental notes to recall when they're finished, so you can hone in on what they're saying to you.*

I'LL HUFF AND PUFF...

Have you ever found yourself trying to resolve the same issues with another person over and over? It seems no matter how **you** try, the two of you can't seem to work it out? I stress the word 'you' because I want to introduce you to a certain personality type I like to call "The Huffer." He or she actually **likes** conflict. They eat, drink, sleep, and breath controversy. It's almost as if they're not happy, unless there's some drama going on. So, they seek to create it where ever they can.

When you come across this person, it's nearly useless to try to resolve the issue, because that's not what they want. But you, being a person who likes harmony, will try everything under the sun, to no avail. It's absolutely exhausting dealing with them and in many cases, you can't get away from them because you may work with them, or they're in your family.

This technique is going to require some discipline ladies, so listen up. As women, we generally want everything to be okay. This places us at a disadvantage when dealing with the huffer because they want the exact opposite outcome. You may ask them, "Is there something bothering you?" To which they respond, "Hmph, no!" You may then ask, "Are you sure? Because you're telling me 'no,' but your body language says something different." They may respond by crossing their arms, rolling their eyes, or making some statement to trigger you like, "You know what you did!" If you have literally run out of ways to get to the bottom of the matter, try using these statements. Be sure to say their name at the beginning of the sentence. *"Kendra, I have exhausted all of my resources to try to resolve this issue with you, and you have made it clear to me that that just isn't something you want. It gives me the impression that you actually **want** the conflict, so…I'm going* *to let you have it. It's yours. I've let it go, and if you ever want to talk to me about settling this matter, I'm open to that.*" Then, you simply smile and walk away.

Here's where the discipline comes in...stop **needing** resolution. When another person knows that you can't be at peace without it, you have just leveraged the power in their favor. You're not going to resolve every issue, with every person. After you make the above statement, walk away and *stay away*. Don't come back another time and ask if they're ready to talk about it. When you do that, it reinforces the fact that you have allowed them to have the control. Only have interaction with them when it's absolutely unavoidable. And even then, don't bring up the issue. Meditate, pray, or do whatever you do to do calm yourself when you feel the urge to revisit the situation.

The huffer normally begins to get irritated when you're not on their heels begging them for their resolution, and so they create new ways to try to aggravate and infuriate you. Unstoppable women can clearly see this childish plan unfold, and she knows better than to be duped by it. See it for what it is, and move on to the things that bring you joy.

Secret: *When it breaks your heart to be at odds with another person, pick up as many pieces as you can to put it back together because women grow stronger in places that were broken.*

IT'S NOT YOU, IT'S THEM...

When trying to resolve conflicts, you may be faced with the exhausting question, "What the heck did I do to them?" To which I say it may not be you at all. You may be searching your brain going through previous interactions and conversations with them trying to pinpoint the experience that triggered the demise of the relationship. Well, allow me to ease your frustrations. It may not be you at all. For example…

For about ten years, I would go and visit a close relative who was incarcerated. Upon entering the facility, you were required to provide your valid identification, vehicle tag number, and turn off cell phones. After the inmate is brought to the visiting area, you then are escorted to the "shake down" room where you're searched to ensure you're not bringing any illegal contraband into the facility. There was a particular guard who was there every time I visited and we'll call her "Paula." Well, Paula would treat me as if I had done something wrong to her. I would get "bad vibes" from her and she would take unnecessary steps to search me in the shake down room. Once I recall her pulling my bra strap and snapping it against the skin on my back like little immature boys used to do when you started wearing training bras. It hurt a little, but I'm not in the habit of making trouble with people who carry weapons ☺. Besides that, I had to be strategic in not allowing any unnecessary hostility to develop wrongfully against my relative. After all, after I leave, he still had to dwell there, so I sucked it up. Comments under the guard's breath were often made in my direction and I just *could not* figure out why I was her chosen target. This went on for years and after weighing all the options, I decided as long as I am granted access to see him and no further complications arise, I can deal with it. My interactions with her were only a few times a year, so compared to other issues in my life, this was relatively small. I did finally ask my relative about it and he stated that he had no idea why she was treating me that way and we both decided to just let it go.

One day I went to visit him and I noticed she wasn't the guard on duty. I immediately felt relief because I wasn't going to have to endure the fiendish treatment. The searching process went smoothly and I was let into the visitation room without any drama. One of the first things I asked him was the whereabouts of Paula. He told me she no longer worked there and before she left, she was transferred to a different post which allowed him to talk to her more often. I inquired again about her disposition and what he told me was astounding.

He said, "Erika, I had an opportunity to talk to her before she left and you will never guess why she didn't like you." My ears felt like they were on fire because I wanted to hear the explanation so badly. He continued, "Remember the incident with the bra? Well, it turns out she had breast cancer and she had to have both of her breasts removed. When she saw you come in, you were a constant reminder of what she no longer had and she resented you for it." I felt my mouth going dry as my jaw dropped at the news. I'm not sure what expression was on my face, but it was enough for him to say, "Hold on Erika, she also wanted me to tell you that she was terribly sorry for the way she treated you and she wanted me to ask you to forgive her." And just like that, I did.

I had no idea what was going on in her world and here I was trying to figure out what role I played in the awkward situation. Sometimes people have issues in their lives and when they see someone who they believe doesn't have those issues, they're resentful. So in essence, sometimes…it really **is** them, not you.

7

He Said, She Said

This chapter was rather fun to write because I'm flooded with all the hilarious memories that I have talking to men about relationships with women. When I'm training a coed group and I get to "Male/Female Dynamics" something in me just radiates. I always look forward to hearing what men have to say. Surprisingly, men are very forthcoming when it comes to saying what's on their minds, contrary to what many women believe. Those being so free with their opinions could be attributed to the fact that they have a sense of reinforcement from the other men in the room, or finally being able to release what they've been wanting to say at home but felt, for whatever reason, they couldn't or shouldn't.

Either way ladies, they *let us have it*! And they should because heaven knows we're not shy when it comes to talking about what's "wrong" with them. But sadly, that's one of the primary issues between the sexes. We talk to our own gender about everything, when we should be talking with our counter-part.

Since the beginning of time we have been studying and analyzing the differences between the male and female species and so far, we've come up with many principles, theories, ideas and strategies. So I'm going to discuss and implement some techniques I've developed through countless hours of group discussions, coaching sessions and on-going learning.

In doing relationship coaching, I ask my female clients to make a list of attributes and characteristics of their ideal mate. I give them a few days to generate the list and when they read the list to me, they speak with such conviction and passion and it's obvious they put a lot thought into it and they appear to be very clear about who it is they desire. After hearing their attributes, I then ask them how long it took to generate the list. On average, it takes approximately 10-45 minutes to create it. Then I ask them if it was relatively easy to come up with the list. For the most part, the ladies revealed it was easy for them because they simply thought of all the issues they experienced in previous and current relationships and they used that as a guidepost. My next question to them is if they would know how to properly handle a relationship with a man that met the qualities on their list. I'm always pleased when I'm given genuine and candid answers. Some ladies say "Yes, I think so" or "I'm not sure" or "I hope so" and "Probably not." Then we go into the why and why not.

The second part of the assessment is to have the ladies generate a second list. On this list they are instructed to record attributes that they *contribute* to a relationship. I give them the same amount of time to complete this list as the first one. But what I've observed is that it takes them longer to complete it, and it's much shorter. I mention the observation to them and one of my clients said to me, "You know, I just know I'm a good woman, but this forced me to define exactly what that means." Why is it so much easier to define what we want from others than it is for us to define what we offer? Often times we think about what we want out of a relationship without giving much thought to what it is we contribute to it.

Unstoppable women are able to state at a moment's notice at least one or two things they have to offer any relationship whether it's business or personal. This stems from having taken inventory of past relationships and how we dealt with them. We've examined what has worked and what hasn't and making a note of it for future reference.

Below you will see two grids of attributes. The first is for you to determine what you want from a relationship. The second is to determine what it is you offer a relationship. Make a copy of it and make sure you have time to sit and think about your choices. This exercise is designed to help you get clear on the direction you want your relationship to go in and how you contribute to that direction. It also helps to have your partner complete the same exercise and compare notes. Do you have the same values? Let's find out.

Directions: Cross out the attributes that are less important to you. *Crossing out the characteristics does not mean that these things aren't important to you.* The object is to discover your **top five** values. So keep crossing things out until you have only five remaining. This will likely be a challenge, so be prepared.

WHAT YOU WANT <u>FROM</u> YOUR RELATIONSHIP

Accomplished In Career	Monogamous	Great Listener	Humble	Supportive
Trust-worthy	Non-Judgmental	Involved Parent	Honest	Protector
Spiritual	Healthy/Fit	Financially Stable	Great Provider	Non Abusive
Goal Oriented	Sexual Compatibility	Great Communicator	Understanding	Romantic
Attentive	Secure with Themselves	Respectful	Sense of Humor	Family Oriented

WHAT YOU HAVE TO <u>OFFER</u> YOUR RELATIONSHIP

Accomplished In Career	Monogamous	Great Listener	Humble	Supportive
Sensitive	Non-Judgmental	Involved Parent	Honest	Gracious
Spiritual	Healthy/Fit	Smart	Great Home Maker	Non Abusive
Resourceful	Sexually Adventurous	Great Communicator	Understanding	Trust-worthy
Good Cook	Secure with Myself	Respectful	Sense of Humor	Speak My Mind

So how did you do? Were you able to complete the exercise without much trouble? I'm guessing it wasn't as easy as you thought it was going to be. The beauty of this grid is that you can add or delete the characteristics as you see fit for both personal and professional relationships.

WHAT DID YOU SAY?!

If you've ever found yourself asking him this question, he likely said something you found appalling or dim-witted. And I'm willing to bet he responded by lifting his shoulders as if to say, "What did I say wrong?" This happens a lot because what he said and what you heard are not in alignment.

"What are you thinking?" Alice asked. To which Jay responded, "Nothing." That drove her nuts! Now what Jay said and what Alice heard are likely two totally different things. Jay was likely thinking, "Nothing important enough to discuss right now." And Alice was thinking, "Something's wrong and he won't tell me. He's shutting me out. Why won't he tell me? Did I do something wrong? Did *he* do something wrong?" What I've learned about men is that sometimes, they actually aren't thinking of anything in particular. As women, we tend to think about everything all the time so it's difficult for us to connect with the idea that they simply aren't thinking about anything.

ARE YOU SURE YOU WANT THE TRUTH?

An old friend of mine Andrea* called me one day to talk about an issue she was having with her husband Joshua*. They'd been married for about five years and she noticed a decline in their sexual activities. Andrea had gained some weight after having children and she feared that her husband wasn't attracted to her anymore. So, she figured she would spice things up but she didn't know where to start. She asked him about some of the things he fantasized about so she could make them come true for him.

He was very reluctant to discuss such things with her, but Andrea pushed and pushed out of sheer desperation to please her husband. Joshua explained that he often fantasized about being part of a ménage á trois but wasn't sure if she'd be interested in trying it. Andrea's heart dropped at the thought of him being with another woman. In addition, she thought that she was the only one he fantasized about. She thought he was going to say something that would involve just the two of them.

Since that conversation, Andrea questioned his every move and even questioned her appearance. She wondered if she was still attractive to him and began starving herself in an attempt to make herself more desirable to him. Despite his desperate pleas, she continued the unhealthy dietary lifestyle and eventually found herself on the floor of the bathroom at work awaiting an ambulance because of her damaging habits. All this was triggered by a simple question. Andrea suffered from major self worth issues and she simply wasn't ready…for the truth.

THE "MAN LIST"

In my never ending quest to better understand the male species, I conducted several dozen group discussions and said to them, "Okay guys, I want you to think of all the things you've ever wanted to say to women and I'm going to put them all on a list. I want you to pretend that *every woman* on the planet is going to read it so don't hold anything back! So tell me, what do you want us to know?" Although there were at least 1,500 men who responded, I observed that the same things kept coming up over and over. I took the top ten things on the list and <u>I'm going to explain their point of views here</u>. Be prepared to dive into the mind of the male species. Ladies, grab a pen…

1. **Get to the Point!-** Men stated that one of their pet peeves is when women ramble on and on about what they perceive as nothing. They think our responses should be succinct and quick. Eric said, "Why can't women just spit it out already?! It's annoying to have to sit there and listen to a high pitched voice say the same things over and over. By the time they get to the third sentence, we've tuned them out." Another man added, "It seems like I'm being lectured to instead of having a conversation. I'm not a little boy."

2. **Support Me 100%-** Men have a lot going on just like we do, and it's important to them to have a solid foundation to help them stay strong in their endeavors. They feel like they have the weight of the world on their shoulders and they need refuge when they come home. I can recall a workshop I attended where the speaker told this story: *A man came home from work one day and his wife asked him if he had completed some tasks she asked him to do. When he replied 'no' she scolded him profusely. He responded by telling her a story. He said to her, "My boss was telling us about his dog that somehow escaped the front yard and ended up in the middle of the street dodging speeding cars trying to get to the other side for safety. He made it across the street without getting hit and realized he had to cross that same street again in order to get back into the safety of his yard. So the dog, scared out of its mind, went back into the street, barely escaping the screeching tires and speeding vehicles and finally made it back into the gates. His wife ran outside and picked up the dog and felt his heart beating rapidly in her arms from the frightful experience. She then proceeded to spank the dog really hard for running out into the street in the first place. What do you think about that?" His wife gasped and covered her mouth and said to him, "Oh, that's awful! Why would she spank the poor dog? She should just be grateful that he wasn't hurt. What an awful thing to do!" To which her husband responded, "That's what you do to me every day. I go out into the world uncertain of how the day will treat me, dodging ill will, facing challenge after challenge, and*

my only refuge is knowing that I will be coming home to be with someone who loves and supports me. But when I get home all I get is a list of things that I failed to do without even considering all that I've endured, much less all the things that I did accomplish." His wife apologized...for the first time in their marriage. Support to them is hard to come by so when they get it from a woman, they cherish it.

3. **Keep Our Relationship Private-** Men get upset when the events of the relationship are broadcast to your friends and family. Some women go as far as to invite the opinions of people outside of the relationship. Keith said, "I'm not in a relationship with your family, I'm with you. There's not enough room for all of us. Not only do I have to deal with you when we have an argument, but I have to deal with your sisters, your mother, your cousins and your friends. It's exhausting." It's difficult to recover from a spat when other people are involved. Outside people are less forgiving than you are when an issue arises. It's understandable to want a support system in place when you're hurting or angry, but the most effective way to resolve the issue is directly with him. If you want to push him away, bringing other people into your relationship is surely a way to do it.

4. **I'm Not a Mind Reader-** Here's where it gets tricky. We want men to know what's going on with us, but we won't tell them. We think he should automatically know if he really cared about us right? Sisters, we couldn't be further

from the truth. When a man *really* cares, he would like for us to convey to him what we're thinking and feeling so he will know how to make it better for us. But it's frustrating to him when we don't talk because he has a feeling of helplessness. Charles told me, "My wife walks around with a chip on her shoulder and when I ask what's wrong, she always says 'If you don't know then you don't care' and that creates a wall of non-communication between us. I love her and want to protect her, but if I don't know what's going on how do I make it better?" There are some things we think they should know like anniversaries, birthdays and other special occasions and when they forget, it gives the impression they are cold or have other priorities. But let's remember #2 on this list. Support them 100%. Maybe there's something going on with them that has created a distraction. Maybe they were passed up for that promotion, maybe the business deal didn't go through as planned, or perhaps they received a bad report from that doctor's visit. Based on what I'm told by men, I suggest that unstoppable women first ask if all is well with them before we get upset. But if all is well ladies…**open your mouth!**

5. **Don't Emasculate Me-** Men will admit that when it comes to having egos, they are likely the more dominant gender. Men want to be all the man you ever need and if there's an area where he falls short, he doesn't want it highlighted, especially in the presence of other people. A perfect example of this is something that a client of mine shared with me. Tina* is a top professional in her field and often times she is called upon to host or entertain clients for her

firm at various black tie events and galas. She has a man in her life named Sam* and they are very happy together. Sam doesn't have as much education as she does, and he doesn't always articulate his thoughts as succinctly, but he is an extremely intelligent, hard-working man who runs his own business. Their line of work is like night and day so Sam doesn't have a lot in common with her colleagues. When he attends the events with her, he's often asked about his line of work and as he speaks, sometimes her colleagues give him a sly look of disapproval. Tina would apologize on his behalf about his lack of verbal communication skills and this angered him immensely. One evening when they got home from an event he confronted her asking her if she was ashamed of him. She replied, "No, I think very highly of you, I just wish your grammar and diction was better." He explained to her in a heated tone, "Regardless of how I talk, you never should embarrass me by apologizing for me like I'm a kid. I know I don't talk that good, but I'm a good man to you and you should appreciate that and love me for who I am." Tina felt awful because he was absolutely right. He gave her practically anything she asked for, provided her with the luxuries of her heart, and loved & supported her while she worked her way up through the company. And that was more precious to her than anything. After they calmed down a few days later, he came to her and asked for her help in correcting his grammar so he could better represent them as a couple in public. He was shocked to hear her say, "Sam, there's nothing wrong with you and I'm so sorry if I gave you any other impression. I was an ass for treating you that way and the opinions of others don't matter to me anymore. You're all that matters." He told her that's all he wanted to hear and from that point on, they worked together on his diction and grammar.

Unstoppable women know how to be tactful and diplomatic when it comes to sensitive issues like this. What Tina could have done to avoid the argument was to share with him any concerns she had and patiently listened to his response to determine how they should proceed. Remember #4 on the list? They are not mind readers.

6. **I'm Not Your Ex-** This one is usually filled with an obvious distaste when men explain it to me. They're very annoyed as they describe how infuriating it is to be treated like the ex-boyfriend or ex-husband. They don't want to be punished for the actions of another man. Kyle explained, "I was with a woman who kept telling me that she's been through 'such-n-such' before and what's-his-name used to do this-n-that to her...It was so annoying." One man even told me he wanted an opportunity to screw things up on his own. He didn't want to be in the shadow of someone who messed up already. So ladies, although it may seem difficult to separate past experiences from present ones, it's important to learn by them, not be confined by them.

7. **Stop Trying to Change Me-** Point blank, men have a good sense of who they are and anything that gives them the impression that that characteristic may be altered will push

them away. Sure, they will put their best foot forward in an effort to impress and woo you, but eventually the more comfortable aspect of their personality will surface and that's the one you'll have to deal with on a day to day basis.

I remember one particular group session when the men were particularly fickle about this topic. Hugh* stated, "Why is it women pretend to accept you for who you are in the beginning, but further into the relationship they disapprove of the very things they said was cute about you?"

So let's examine that for a moment ladies. Are you guilty of leading him to believe that his habits are acceptable to you just so you can "land" him and then complaining about those habits? I asked for examples of behaviors and/or characteristics that were no longer acceptable to their women and here's a short list of what they provided:

- I'm messy
- I go to strip clubs
- I play video games
- I watch sports (A lot!)
- I'm a workaholic
- I hang out with my friends
- I drink
- I smoke
- I don't dance
- I'm over-weight

When you're dating, you may feel a "spark" and you don't want to rock the boat so you pretend that these things don't bother you so you don't come off as a whiny complainer. Don't want to scare him away right? Well, let's look at #4 on this list. They like it when you're forthcoming about your likes and dislikes as long as it's said in a fashion that isn't emasculating (#5 on the list) Hmmm, it seems a lot of this is tied together doesn't it? It is ladies!

8. **Don't Change Who You Were-** In this instance men wonder what happened to the woman they first met and want her back. A perfect example is Ted and Rosalyn. They met at a ball park and the only reason Rosalyn was there is because she lost a bet with a friend. She hated baseball. But when she met Ted, she lied and told him she loved the sport just so she could have something in common with him. As time went on, her visits to the ball park with him got fewer and fewer and finally she had to break down and tell him she didn't care for the sport. This greatly disappointed Ted; he was a baseball fanatic and the fact that he met her there was one of the reasons he was so drawn to her. He said, "Even if she had told me the truth in the beginning, I wouldn't have forced her to go with me. I love the sport and knowing she'd be miserable there wouldn't make it very enjoyable for either of us. I fell in love with her because I thought we shared a common bond in that area. Now I feel like I don't know her at all."

A more common example is sexual activity. Men express frustration when they describe how the sex was when they first got together and how it dissipated dramatically after a certain length of time. Larry said, "Don't they know that what they do in the beginning is what we want from them all the time? Granted, it may not be spectacular each time, but don't cut off the good stuff altogether." Men admit that they think about sleeping with another woman when the sex with their committed partner begins to fade, but most of them agree that if the activity was more of what they became accustomed to in the beginning, they would think less of women outside of their relationship.

9. **Let Me Know I'm Needed and Wanted-** When I first heard this I immediately thought I asked the wrong question. But in the midst of the conversation, it became quite clear what they meant. Some women say, "I don't need a man!" That's one of the biggest turn-offs for men to hear. They figure, "If you don't need me for anything, why even bother?" Men want to be the protectors, the providers and the advisors and when one or more of these areas aren't being solicited, they lose interest in the relationship because they don't think they serve a purpose. They want you to ask for their opinions so they can help you solve a problem. They want to keep you safe and create a sense of protection when they're around. And they want to give you the desires of your heart. So if you were to say, "I don't need you for *anything*," they're knee jerk reaction is to seek someone who will call upon them for the above mentioned strengths.

10. **Do Not Smother Me-** A man likes when a woman has some things in her life that she's interested in outside of him. This makes time to miss each other. Women who are too needy turn men off in a major way. They want to be the provider, not the father. David told me, "My girlfriend calls me at least ten times a day just to see what I'm thinking and it got on my damn nerves. When I walk in the door, she's all over me. When I'm on the phone, she wants me to hang up so I can give her some attention. She doesn't want kids because she thinks it'll take too much time away from us. What the hell!?"

You remember those things we mentioned before about the habits and characteristics men have when you first get together ladies? They like to be awarded freedom to do those things without guilt. And what kind of life can you possibly have if it's consumed with his every move? Your self esteem is seriously challenged if your world revolves around him, so for the sake of your sanity and the relationship…get a life!

I also asked men what it is about women that stimulated them mentally. One gentleman said, "Women have to understand that men are very visual creatures. Initially it's the looks that get our attention, but there has to be some substance in order to *keep* our attention."

So these are the top things on their list and there were other issues that they mentioned, but I wanted to provide you with the ones that can essentially be deal breakers.

Now, it wouldn't be fair to mention the things on a man's list if I didn't mention a few things on women's list. So here are the top ten on our list:

1. **Listen to Me-** We want them not only to hear us, but to absorb the message we're trying to convey.

2. **Communicate with Me-** It's imperative that they convey their thoughts and feelings so we'll know how to manage the situation.

3. **Support Me in My Interests-** To provide us with feedback, ideas or observations about our interests is important. If we want to start a business, don't be jealous. If we are stay-at-home mothers, help me make the home more comfortable.

4. **Check Your Ego at the Door-** Basically, understand that just because you're a man doesn't mean you have complete control. Respect the fact that I'm a woman and I have my own thoughts and ideas.

5. **Don't Be Abusive-** Don't ever abuse me emotionally, physically, mentally or otherwise.

6. **Be Loyal-** Women prefer men who are reliable, trustworthy, and dedicated to the growth of the relationship.

7. **Have Some Ambition-** Women have stated they like a man who has goals and actually pursues them as opposed to simply talking about them.

8. **Be Chivalrous-** Treat me like a lady.

9. **Protect Us from Harm-** Nearly 88% of women I talked to stated that this is an important factor in the foundation of a relationship. What's even more interesting is that at least 50% of them admit they don't like feeling that way.

10. **Don't Judge Me-** I remember Tara said, "I told my ex-husband about a few past experiences and he treated me differently ever since. I was reluctant to share, but since he asked and I wanted to build a stronger bond, I shared them with him. That was the biggest mistake I'd ever made with him."

An observation I've made is the irony between the #1 point on each list. For men, it was "**Get to the Point**," and for women it was "**Listen to Me**." (Read that again) See a conflict?

> One of the best ways to reduce conflict
> is say what you want from the conversation up front.
>
> *"I don't want you to solve my problem,*
> *I just need a sounding board so just listen."*

WORKPLACE WOES

I want to discuss dealing with men on a more professional level. There are some simple things women can do to create a balance in the workplace. Let's start with the language we choose. As women we have a tendency to use the words "I feel." When men hear this, they immediately think that we're too emotional and we can't handle pressure and that we'll fall apart. And it's completely untrue, but there's a way to alter it to give a different impression. First, replace the words *"I feel"* with *"It gives me the impression."* Here's an example of what I mean:

Carly believes that her colleague Ralph doesn't think very highly of her because she's a woman. In addressing this issue, Carly said, "Ralph, I feel like you don't respect me and that you feel my ideas are stupid and I resent that." Resentment is an emotion so avoid using them as much as possible. Instead, Carly can say, "Ralph, when you make snide remarks and laugh when I present my ideas, it gives me the impression that you don't respect my views or opinions and that you don't see me as an asset to this team." Two things have happened here. First, she completely removed the emotional aspect of the situation by eliminating the words "I feel" and not mentioning an emotion. Second, she provided a solid example of specific behaviors he displayed so he would understand that she is clear about the behavior she's addressing.

Standing up for yourself in a diplomatic fashion earns you respect in the workplace. There are some prejudices against women in the workplace such as:

- Women fall apart under pressure
- Women are too emotional
- Women can't separate work and personal issues
- Women gossip too much
- Women have difficulty making tough decisions
- Women allow themselves to be walked over

This is a very short list of many. But, there's a way we can dispel these myths bit by bit. I'm reminded of a tricky situation where the head of the company, Mr. Evans*, had asked for ideas on how to deal with a dilemma our company was experiencing. We were to present these ideas at the next meeting. I was perplexed about possible solutions and as I was having lunch, I was conversing with a colleague named Jason* and all of a sudden an idea hit me. I was so excited about it that I just started talking without considering possible consequences. Jason's face lit up at the idea and figured it would work. Later that afternoon was the meeting and when Mr. Evans opened the floor for new ideas, Jason instantly began talking about my idea but he was explaining it as if it was his own suggestion. Mr. Evans thought it was an excellent idea and I found myself faced with two options. I could sit back and allow Jason to accept full credit for my idea and let the fact that the company would benefit be my reward. Or, I could speak up and claim the rights to my brainchild. But in choosing that route, I had to do so in a manner that wouldn't seem malicious, emotional, or selfish. I had little time to waste so I chose the second option. I smiled at Jason and said, "Jason, I'm so glad you agree with me because when I explained this idea to you earlier today, I wasn't sure how well it would be received. (Then I turned my eyes to the rest of the room) Another aspect I considered since Jason and I talked was..." This let everyone in the room know that the idea was mine and it also revealed Jason as someone who takes credit for the ideas of others.

It will take some practice replacing emotional verbiage with less sensitive ones. I suggest utilizing a thesaurus and expand your vocabulary to better articulate your thoughts. With some effort and dedication to the process, we might just put to rest the seemingly constant battle between the sexes once and for all. But it will take patience, understanding, and above all, respect to make this happen.

The bottom line is this: Unstoppable women make it their business to understand how a man thinks so she can better strategize her plans to suit her goals. Sounds manipulative? To manipulate, you achieve your goals at the expense of others by *using them*. These techniques are not intended for that. Instead, it's a guide to assist you in being a well respected and valued woman in their world, business or personal.

8

Mirror, Mirror

The deepest form of reflection never involves a mirror. In this chapter, my goal is to get you to look deep within yourself and analyze why you have made the choices you made and use this information to make better ones. In retrospect, I have had some pretty remarkable experiences. Some I loved, some I wish never to repeat. But I have no regrets because every single choice I made has brought me to this point and I love the woman I have become.

When I speak at conferences, or when I conduct trainings, I'm often perceived as a woman who has everything under control. One participant in my group challenged me publicly saying, "But how would *you* know what it's like to struggle with real issues? You're successful, attractive and you seem to have an answer for everything. I don't find that very credible." I should mention that this was a multi-day seminar and this participant missed the first day when I revealed personal stories of hardship. But nevertheless, it got me thinking. In order to relate to the lives of people, I have to expose <u>my</u> life to them. So here, in this book, I will share some horrific, enlightening, and liberating experiences that have shaped the life I now lead. Take from them what you will, and seek the message.

THE MIGRAINES

It's interesting how you don't take notice of things until they're gone. Or in my case, I hadn't realized how good I had it until something undesirable showed up. Here's what I mean…

I got married in 2004 and before that, I had never gotten a headache in my life. It wasn't something I bragged about or anything, it just wasn't something I had experienced. My marriage

144

was very stressful to me and about six months or so into my marriage, I felt a strange "twinge" in my head and couldn't figure out what it was. I know it sounds ridiculous, but the idea of it being a headache never even crossed my mind. I kept thinking, "Did I hit my head? Was my wig on too tight?" I ignored it in hopes it would go away, but it didn't. The following day I felt a little better when I woke up in the morning, but as the day progressed, it got worse. Finally I figured it might be a headache and so I took some over the counter pain reliever and it worked. "Wow," I thought. "My first headache!"

Why I thought that was something to be proud of I'll never know. But unbeknownst to me, things were about to get much worse. The headaches came more and more frequently over time, and got stronger. I found myself popping more pills than I ever have in my life. One day I simply could not open my eyes because the light hurt me so badly. I was at my best friend's house laying in her daughter's bed when she came in and rubbed my temples for me. She's a registered nurse and while she massaged my head she advised me to see a doctor. So, I did just that.

The doctor sent me to a neurologist to get to the bottom of my frequent headaches. My husband came along with me and the doctor ran some tests. I remember my husband stepped out of the room and the doctor said to me, "Mrs. Williams, you're much too young to have this level of discomfort so frequently. I don't know what *or who* is stressing you out, but if you don't get a handle on it, it's going to get much worse and the damage could be irreversible."

145

When he emphasized the words "*or who*" it was as if he knew the root of my stress, but chose not to state it. Within months, I left my husband. Today, I still get headaches, but they're very manageable and far less frequent. I'll certainly take that over what I experienced during my marriage.

> ## What we should do has already been revealed to us. The question is...WHEN will we actually do it?

Have you ever felt so distraught that you didn't think that things could get any worse? Whatever your situation is, there's somebody else who would gladly trade places with you to get out of their circumstances. Let's look at it this way: In Chicago it can easily get below zero during the winter months. But sometimes, we make it into the 40's and when we do, we say "Man, it is really warm outside!" But in the summertime, if it was in the 40's we would say that it was very cold. The temperature itself hasn't changed, just our perspective based on the conditions surrounding it. Therefore, when you believe that you're the only one who has experienced what you're feeling, you're both right and incorrect. No one can have the exact same emotions as you because they haven't experienced the exact same thing you have since your birth. However, they can experience the same situation, causing them to have similar emotions.

PUTTING IT ALL IN PERSPECTIVE

I was working full time, making a handsome salary, able to save money, pay my bills and I had great health benefits. Sounds like a great deal right? Well, I failed to mention a few things about this job. It was a two-hour commute each way, I worked 10-16 hour shifts, I was responsible for four locations and 30+ staff members, it was physically grueling, I got very little sleep, and my stress level skyrocketed.

I was in that position for a while working diligently, staying focused, and not giving much attention to anything else until one day I noticed I started spotting. Immediately it dawned on me that I hadn't had my cycle in at least two months and I made an appointment to see a doctor in the next few weeks. The bleeding got more severe and after two visits to the emergency room I was told that the test results revealed there was nothing wrong with me. I returned to work thinking that perhaps my cycle was just a bit heavier because of the new stress on my body from all the new hustle and bustle of work.

This particular day I can remember like it happened just ten minutes ago. I was talking to my supervisor about a new window display when all of a sudden I felt a wave of warm liquid flood my pants and I immediately excused myself to the ladies room. I was bleeding profusely and I started to get light-headed. I didn't have my cell phone so I had to walk back to the store and have my staff call an ambulance. I could barely stand due to the dizziness and finally when the paramedics arrived, they wheeled me away to the waiting ambulance. Upon arriving at the hospital, the doctors and nurses examined me and revealed I was hemorrhaging and the doctor stated I needed to have emergency surgery immediately. I had a miscarriage and a D & C (Dilation & Curettage) prior to this incident and I later learned that the D & C was not performed properly which caused the hemorrhaging.

After the surgery, I was resting in the recovery room when the doctor entered and sat next to me. I don't ever recall a doctor sitting down next to me before and it really stood out. She smiled at me and asked how I was feeling to which I replied, "A little weak, but otherwise okay." What she said to me next will forever be burned in my memory. "You lost quite a bit of blood and if you'd have waited just a couple more hours bleeding the way you were, we wouldn't have been able to save you. You would've bled to death."

Without saying a word, I nodded and turned my head away to process what was just revealed to me. I suppose I could have been thinking about malpractice lawsuits and the embarrassment of being hauled away in front of my staff and a bunch of other things, but all I could feel was an overwhelming sense of gratitude. When something like that is revealed to you, you get really clear about your priorities real damn quick.

IT'S NOT AS BAD AS IT SEEMS

I interviewed for a job as a Store Manager at a major airport. I'll admit that trying to get this job was one of the most peculiar processes I'd ever experienced in landing a position. The day of my interview I missed all three trains by just a few moments, the terrible weather caused a rail malfunction and the trains were delayed, I got my suit pants wet, and I was late. I thought for sure my chances of being hired were shot.

After arriving 20 minutes late, out of breath, and dirty, I sat down to two interviewers who did not make it a secret that they were displeased with me thus far. I proceeded through the interview as if I was on-time, neatly pressed, and unshaken by their disapproving glares. The interview lasted approximately 20-30 minutes and at the end, they asked me about my salary requirements. At this point I'm thinking they must like me because who asks that question if they're not interested? So I reached down in my sack of courage and pulled out a number I knew for sure they'd decline. They looked at each other as if to say, "Is she serious?" and extended their hand, ending the interview.

I left the interview feeling pretty good despite all the drama that occurred prior to it. The ride home wasn't nearly as rough. The weather subdued, I caught every train just in time, my pants dried out and I arrived home earlier than I anticipated. After I changed clothes and sat down to a nice meal, I noticed that my voicemail indicator was illuminated on my cell phone. I hadn't heard it ring, so a call must have come through while I was underground on the train. I checked the message and it was one of the interviewers calling to extend the position to me at the salary I asked for.

If I focused on the issues I experienced on my way there, I would easily believe that I didn't have a chance at landing that position. But instead, I concentrated on how I overcame them and shifted the tone of the interview.

So what does reflection have to do with being unstoppable? Reflection allows you take into account the experiences and lessons you've learned and apply them to your present situations and circumstances to provide a guidepost to assist in your navigation to your desired destination. In simpler terms, it allows you to look back to gauge the direction of your next step.

It's okay to take a look at things that didn't go well so you can assess what to do differently, but *don't stay there*. Unstoppable women understand this concept all too well. The sooner you learn to reflect, apply, and release (R.A.R.), the faster you'll become unstoppable.

JUST DO WHAT YOU DO

I've always been an artistic being and expressing myself came easily when I was surrounded by others who I felt were like me. It was joyous and liberating to be comfortable dancing, goofing off, and reciting lines from my favorite movies and poems without fear of being ridiculed and laughed at.

It wasn't until high school that I realized that not everyone appreciated artistic people. The school wasn't exactly a pleasant place for me. I had never experienced such a strong distaste for being different from everybody else. I wasn't accustomed to it so I embraced a small population of students who I felt understood who

I was. I didn't feel the need to fit in with everybody, I just wanted to feel comfortable with *somebody*. Fortunately, I was able to identify with a small group of people who were in my drama class (how appropriate right?). I learned improve, stage direction, breathing exercises, and how to "get into character." I absolutely loved it! I could be a 40 year old gas station attendant on Monday, and a wealthy 80 year old heiress on Wednesday.

One day my drama teacher announced that we were going to perform in front of the entire school for black history month. Each drama student was given a project, and I was assigned a solo dance number in honor of Sam Cooke. I kept thinking, "Why couldn't I have been given one of the backstage assignments? I don't want to dance by myself in front of all these unappreciative people." But, this was going to count towards our grade, and I wasn't about to let anyone interfere with my GPA.

Although I love to dance, I was less than eager to do this particular performance. Minutes before I was to go on stage, I did a quick appearance check in the mirror. I wore a long, ankle length yellow dress with a satin yellow sash, an over-sized yellow hat, a large yellow hand fan, and I was in my bare feet. I took a deep breath and walked out onto the stage.

I could hear the grunts, laughter, and callous remarks my classmates were making as I took my first position. Between that and the knots in my stomach, I could barely hear the music when it started. The song "Summer Time" by Sam Cooke played over the speakers and I began to move and the only thing I could think about was when this song was going to end.

In order to finish the routine, I had to completely block out the boos, loud chatters, and meaningless white noises. All I could hear was the music, and all I could feel was my body moving through the choreography in perfect sync. After what seemed like 20 minutes, the song ended and I ran off the stage horrified. I ran so fast that my hat flew off and I dropped the fan. I was determined to run until I got to the dressing room where I thought for sure I was going to be sick. A sudden jerk to my right arm snapped me out of my trance. It was my drama teacher stopping me in mid sprint to get my attention. She looked me in the eyes and pointed toward the stage I just left and she said, "Erika, stop running!!!! Listen..."

I was looking down at the floor and turned my focus to my sense of hearing. All of the booing, laughing and demeaning remarks turned into thunderous applause and whistling. I couldn't believe my ears! I turned slowly, still in disbelief and gradually walked back toward the stage with an expression of "is this true?" on my face. As I reappeared on stage, the audience stood to their feet and the roaring cheers grew even louder. My hand immediately found its way to my chest as the realization sank in that they actually enjoyed my performance. I took a bow, waved at the crowd and exited the stage. My classmates greeted me offstage with clapping and pats on the back. It was one of the most exhilarating moments of my life.

The next day I was in my electronics class sitting alone in the corner like I always did that period just waiting for the bell to ring. It wasn't my favorite class to be in because it was filled with highly unmotivated students who just wanted to get by. Many of them were affiliated with some type of gang or illicit behavior. I never felt like I fit in there so sitting in the corner was comfortable for me. I was reading a book when I noticed movement out of the corner of my eye. I glanced up and one of the school's most notorious gang members was walking towards me. He couldn't have been approaching anyone else, because I was the only one in that part of the room. I felt my heart pounding profusely in my chest and for a brief moment, I think I stopped breathing.

He reached my desk and without saying a word, he firmly placed both of his hands on top of it and glared down at me. I hadn't realized how substantially large he was until that moment. It was like staring into the eyes of a giant. I forced a swallow in an attempt to get rid of the lump in my throat, and looked up at him as if to say, "Yes?" He took a quick fleeting look around the room to see if anyone was within ear shot, turned his gaze back to me with a tiny, nearly unnoticeable smile and said, "Hey, you did a great job yesterday…very inspiring, I got a little choked up. That took a lot of guts to get up there in front of all those people. I'm proud of you." Then in the same breath the smile diminished when he added, "Don't tell anybody I told you that." I mimed the "cross my heart" sign and smiled in relief. Without saying anything else, he winked at me, turned and walked away.

I had no idea the impact I had on him. And I thought to myself, "Whoa! I never would've guessed..." I'm sure it wasn't easy for him to express to me how he was affected by my performance. He was the least likely individual, in my opinion, to be touched by something like that. It was then when I understood the power of doing what you love to do with passion. He was just one person out of hundreds who actually said something. Who knows how many other individuals were equally moved. From then on I decided to see myself as an influential being who can assist in the evolution of others by simply doing what I love to do.

Secret: *Regardless of whether or not you're acknowledged for your work, keep doing what you love to do passionately and the appreciation will come.*

DO YOU LIKE ME?

I was visiting my best friend some years back and my niece climbed into my lap, placed her hands on my cheeks (I love it when she did that) and asked me, "Auntie, do you like me?" It wasn't expected and I paused to try to figure out where that question came from. I looked at her and said, "Sweetheart, I *love* you." She huffed, rolled her eyes and stated, "I know that, but do you LIKE me?"

It took the question of a six year old for me to really internalize the distinction between the two. By definition, I knew the difference, but I always assumed that everyone (including myself) knew how to make that determination. Look at yourself in the mirror and ask yourself if you like who you see. It's not enough to just love yourself. It's important to *like* who you are as well. If you don't like who you see staring back at you, the chances of you being truly fulfilled are very slim. However, the good news is that it's never too late to become the woman you've always wanted to be.

YOUR PERCEPTION OF CHANGE

I recall sitting in a seminar when the speaker told this very simple story: *There was a man who lived in a heavily populated city. He had a job, he had a car, and an apartment. One day, his place of work made some dramatic changes and it altered his life significantly. He now drives a different car, he lives someplace else, and he holds a different position at work.*

That's the end of the story. Now, one of two things just happened. In your mind, either you visualized that man getting a promotion, upgrading his car, and moving to nicer place, or you figured he was demoted, downgraded his vehicle, and moved into a less desirable apartment. The story never stated if the changes at his job were good or bad. So then, I have to ask you...which scenario did your mind depict? The answer to this question brings us to the ultimate question: ***How do you perceive change?*** Is it frightening, intimidating and scary? Or is it exciting, hopeful, and adventurous?

It's perfectly natural to be cautious when it comes to change, but consider this: Change is necessary in the growth of the human spirit. It's certainly crucial in the journey to being unstoppable. Don't be afraid of change. Many women take the "safe" route each opportunity because taking risks could mean change. And certainly it will, but look at all the remarkable possibilities it presents. If you perceive change as a dire, grim, frightful experience, then you're the one who's getting in the way of being unstoppable. Change your perception, and you will change your life!

THE AWAKENING

Late one night I woke up from a dream that was both disturbing and enlightening. The luminous being I was created to be was revealed to me in that dream. While the emotions from the dream were still prevalent, I quickly grabbed a pen and paper and started writing from that place of duality. What I wrote that night is featured on the following page.

MIRROR, MIRROR

Mirror, mirror in my hand,
how do I survive this land?
To be a woman who's truly free;
to be the woman I've always wanted to be?
To see myself for who I really am
and embrace her and love her again & again.
To dispel the myths bestowed upon me,
and rid myself of the bureaucracy.
To love my eyes, my legs, my heart & mind,
my flaws & my quirks I've developed over time.
To look beyond what I think I see,
At the blinding light that shines within me.
To close my eyes and still see who I am,
And embrace the grandeur
I have come to understand.
To finally see the love that's
always belonged to me,
And accept it & share it wholeheartedly.
Through all this madness I have
drawn the conclusion
that my imperfections are just an illusion.
Because unconditional love
is not a fallacy.
It's all there is, all there was,
And all there ever will be...

So when you reflect on your past experiences, what lessons do you see? What changes would you like to make? And more importantly, would you want to experience it again? If your answer is no, then make decisions that steer you in the opposite direction. Embrace who you are, and the woman you will become. Each day is a day closer to that manifestation, so have some patience with yourself. You don't have to be "Superwoman" to be a super woman!

9

Who Do You Think You Are?

"Just who do you think you are?" When asked that question in my adolescence, it was meant as a way of saying "You're not special." But as an adult it would behoove us to answer it literally. Do you think you're outstanding, vibrant, smart, funny, dynamic and pleasant? Or do you think you're uninspiring, off-putting, dull, incompetent, unworthy and self loathing? Answering this question honestly puts you in a great place to navigate your life according to where you'd like it to be.

Let's start with examining a common myth that smothers our society. Being successful and happy is generally measured by how much you obtain and/or accomplish. It is believed that the more you have, the happier you'll be. Attaining life's luxuries and being part of an elite circle gives many people a strong sense of self worth. It's a natural thing to do, but it can be detrimental and I challenge that idea just as strongly.

YOU HAVE IT ALL...NOW WHAT?

Let's assume you had many luxuries. What if you have a beautiful newly built home, a partner or spouse, children, a great paying job with benefits and every car you've always wanted to have. Would that make you happy?

One of my colleagues, Gina* had all of those things and then some. She worked in corporate America for 28 years in the technology industry. This was a male dominated industry and she was reminded of that every single day.

Despite all the monetary luxuries she and her husband possessed, she was extremely unhappy. She always wanted to motivate and inspire people; something that simply did not happen in the industry she was in. But she continued to stay in it because of the money. Whenever she would speak of leaving her job, her husband, friends, and her parents horribly gasped at her, asking her if she was crazy.

She talked about how Sundays were incredibly depressing for her because she knew she had to go to work the next day. She had plenty of money and was absolutely miserable. Money simply wasn't a big enough motivator anymore. She looked at her paycheck one day and felt no enthusiasm or inspiration at all. Then she woke up one day and realized she was getting older and she was living a dull, listless existence.

She had enough. She wanted to live a life of passion and meaning so she quit the cushy job, departed from her husband, and got a much smaller house. It wasn't an easy move to make, but in hindsight, it wasn't that difficult either. She now expresses how elated she is with her current lifestyle and how she's filled with a sense of happiness and fulfillment on a daily basis. She said, "I wake up with a renewed sense of energy because I'm living my purpose!"

Secret: *Unstoppable women don't measure success by the number of things they accumulate.*

Ask yourself if you're genuinely happy with your current lifestyle. Is there something else you'd rather be doing? Are you settling for what's convenient instead of what's purposeful? You really deserve the life you truly desire and it's yours, if you go get it!

> *"Without self-respect, there can be no genuine success. Success that is won at the cost of self-respect is not success."*
>
> *- B.C. Forbes*

So, how much **do** you think you're worth? Don't bother looking in your bank account, instead look deeply within and assess your personal level of self esteem. For many of us it's a difficult thing to do because we have a mythical impression of what it means to be worthy of something. I will clarify what it means to have self worth, but first let's look at some dangerous myths surrounding it.

As you consider what your self worth is, you may take into consideration some aspects of your life to help you better assess it. You may have considered your physical appearance, your level of education, the current status of your relationship, your skills and more. These things are not determining factors of your value.

The following is a list of common factors that are usually used to measure personal value, but should not be used:

- Educational level
- Employment status
- Accomplishments/Achievements
- Physical abilities
- Your ability to perform certain skills
- Your personal relationships
- Your marital status

- Your physical appearance
- Your income
- Your friends or social circle
- Your parental status

Trying to improve your self esteem by improving these areas of your life set you up for failure because the moment an unexpected crisis occurs that threatens or destroys any of these areas, your self esteem is also threatened or destroyed. Certainly a high-paying job, a great marriage, higher education, ideal physical appearances and having well behaved children will give you a sense of self worth, but they are not the source. These things may be very important to you, but don't depend on them to make you feel good about yourself; they are after all, cosmetic. You are not valuable *because* of these things; you are valuable *in spite* of them.

SO WHAT IS SELF WORTH?

Self worth is the value you place on yourself simply because you are a human being and **knowing you deserve** all that your heart desires. In this chapter I will show you how to build your self worth without requiring certain accomplishments or obtaining a particular status. This is not to say that you won't create accomplishments, higher education, better friends, and better relationships as a result of having higher self worth. You just won't be so dependent on these things to define who you are. How you view yourself essentially determines how you deal with circumstances and conditions of your existence. There are many aspects of life that have contributed to how you view yourself.

Below you will see a list of some of these things:

So how do you start building your self worth? Start by giving yourself a number between 1 and 10 with 10 being an impeccable level of self worth, and 1 being practically no self worth at all. It's okay to take a moment or two before you come up with a number. If you have chosen any number lower than a 10, I have some good news for you! This chapter will show you ways of boosting your self worth so you can be a much happier you.

THE SOURCE OF SELF WORTH

To put it as simply as possible, YOU are the source of your self worth. Think about how many times have you been in some of the most undesirable positions and you needed help. You looked around for somebody...*anybody* to help you, and the only person you saw was you. At those moments you have a choice. You can be your worst enemy, or you can be your best ally. Let's look at how you can be your own ally.

It begins with what you allow yourself to think and feel. You may allow self deprecating thoughts to enter your mind because of past experiences of which you have not let go. Although they may have been very painful, you prevent better experiences from entering your life when you refuse to let go of them. Here are some exercises you can do to begin the process of letting go.

Exercise #1: Grab as many ink pens or pencils as you can hold in one hand. Make sure they aren't sentimental or valuable to you because you will be throwing them away. With each painful experience that you continuously allow yourself to think of and relive, pick up one item. As you pick up each one, say out loud, "This pen represents the time when…" Keep picking them up until your hand is so full, you can't place any more in. Now walk over to a trash can, hold your hand over the opening and drop them in all at once while saying, "I release you from my life and I will never pick you up again." Repeat this process as many times as necessary until you have released all of the painful experiences you can think of.

Exercise #2: With some washable markers, write something that consumes you with low self worth on each limb. Perhaps on your left arm you can write "losing weight" and on your right leg you can write "low income" and so on. Now step into the shower and adjust the water as warm as you can stand it without being uncomfortable. Using your favorite soap or cleanser, wash away each limb and say out loud, "As you flow from my skin, you flow from my life, down the drain and never to be seen again."

What's unique about these exercises is that they can be repeated on a daily basis as often as you need until you are free of the hold they've had on you.

YOU ARE MORE THAN CAPABLE

Below you will see a list of statements. Place a checkmark next to the ones that describe you in <u>any</u> aspect of your life. You want to be as honest as you can, but be mindful not to be too hard on yourself.

_____ I can communicate my thoughts and feelings effectively

_____ I am sensitive to the feelings of others

_____ I know I am deserving of better things

_____ I think about success often

_____ I try to help people as often as I can

_____ I love listening to music that makes me feel good

_____ I surround myself with people who love me

_____ If I shop for others, sometimes I pick something up for

myself as well

_____ I am good at something

_____ I carve out "me" time in my schedule

_____ It takes a lot to get me upset

_____ I can see my role in conflict

_____ I accept compliments graciously

_____ I'm capable of letting go of past experiences that were
hurtful

_____ I'm often sought after for advice

If you checked **11-15** statements, that terrific! Your self worth is on an awesome track. If you checked **6-10** statements, you have a rich blend of strengths and some areas remaining to build. If you checked **0-5** statements, you're in an exceptional position because you are holding this book in your hands as a very powerful tool that will assist you in all aspects of your life.

SELF WORTH IN ACTION

One of my former clients, Cyleste*, experienced an ordeal that changed her life forever. She's a mother of two, and a disciplined military career woman. After getting into a relationship with Ronald*, she thought it was something really special. He did all the right things and said things that made her feel loved and safe.

One day on a romantic getaway trip, she began to sense a dramatic change in his behavior. He displayed strong characteristics of someone who desired to control her. When she resisted, he became physically violent and brutally beat her until she was unconscious.

169

After the ordeal, she was hospitalized and eventually found herself in a women's shelter feeling like a statistic. A friend of hers kept her children while her physical wounds healed. She didn't want her children to see her in that state. Although most of the wounds were healed, there was some permanent physical damage to her face and it was pretty obvious. She speculated if people at work knew about what happened to her. She wondered how she was going to explain how she looked to her staff. After all, she was a health care provider and many people looked up to her. Even scarier was the thought of explaining it to her children.

Celeste simply didn't want to cope with *anything*. She didn't even want to get out of bed. She fell into a deep depression and soon realized that she was giving Ronald power over her. She had stopped her life because of an ordeal that wasn't her fault. With this realization, she began to heal and she went through therapy. While she was there she developed a strong sense of self value. She told me, "It was an undeniable truth. God's love was stronger than any blow he could have hit me with." Celeste gathered her courage and no longer wondered how she was going to explain her situation. She simply knew that she had to move forward.

She sat her two children down and explained to them what happened. When she talked to her daughter, she pointed at her face and said, "You deserve better than this. This is not love and any person who does this to you does not love you." To her son she explained, "You never treat women like this. Always remember to care for women the same way you'd want someone to care for me."

Due to procedure, her supervisor, Mike*, was told about the situation. Celeste and Mike didn't get along well and always bumped heads at work and the thought of him knowing what happened further humiliated her. But something extraordinary happened. He responded immediately by coming to her to ensure she was okay. He was gracious, caring, and genuinely concerned. Celeste even said he was "human." She couldn't quite figure out why his behavior towards her was so different now. Was it pity? She despised that thought. But soon, she got her answer. He revealed to her that when he was a child, he witnessed first hand the abuse his mother had endured. He talked about how powerless he felt as a young boy and he sincerely wanted to help Celeste.

So, I asked Celeste, "What made you get out of the relationship and press charges?" Her statement was simple and prevailing. She stated, "Because I deserved better." She went on to explain how in the middle of the night she looked around at her unfamiliar environment in the women's shelter and asked herself how she got there. And the answer rang as true as the light of day. She allowed herself to feel less than she actually was, therefore, allowing others to do the same.

Once you have that moment of "knowingness," that undeniable sense of self worth, you start to kick ass and take names. Anyone who has been treating you like you were less than human get to experience the inevitable result of being banished from your life. It's an overwhelming and exhilarating sensation when you square your shoulders and rightfully step into the shoes of the

unstoppable woman you've always been. Even when you look at yourself in the mirror, you see a completely transformed being that looks back at you, nods her head approvingly as if to say, "I knew you had it in you! Welcome to the woman you've always wanted to be."

> "They cannot take away our self respect if we do not give it to them."
> - Mahatma Gandhi

TAKE OUT THE TRASH

Growing up, my grandmother ensured the house was clean by delegating household chores to each of us in the house. There were particular chores I didn't mind doing like mopping the floor and vacuuming the carpet. Then there were chores I actually liked doing like doing laundry and ironing. But some household chores were (and still is) simply dreadful for me. I've never liked washing dishes and taking out the trash. I'm not sure why those particular tasks were so ghastly for me, but the distaste didn't disappear as I got older. To this day, I absolutely cannot stand washing dishes and taking out the trash.

Although I dislike doing these things, I know it's necessary to perform these tasks because if I don't do them, the house begins to smell, and unwanted pests appear (one thing I can't stand more than washing dishes is pests). So I suck it up and get the job done for clean, desirable living conditions.

The same rules apply to your life. There are some challenges you may not mind tackling and others you may enjoy taking on. And then there are obstacles that simply cause you to shrivel up and run in the opposite direction. Ladies, it's time to take out the trash. It's time to take on the chores, challenges, and undesirable situations head-on to get to the other side. The best way out is always directly through it. So, when you have poisonous people in your life, who you know should have been extricated a long time ago but weren't, for whatever reason, here's how you begin the process:

- Delete their number from your phone- When scrolling through your phone, if you come across their name, you may be tempted to call. Or, change their name to "***Do Not Answer***."

- Get rid of the gifts they gave you- Those teddy bears, trinkets, cards, and other items they gave you will immediately remind you of them. Remember the saying 'out of sight, out of mind.'

- Toss the old photographs- Nothing brings back memories like a picture. This will likely be the toughest deletion of your life. There are two ways to do this. You can have a "cleansing" ceremony where you take the pictures and recite positive affirmations as you tear them and throw them away. Another way is to gather them all together, place them into an envelope, and drop them into the mailbox addressed to "The Universe."

- Stop inquiring about them to mutual friends- Unless they bring the person up, steer clear of mentioning them.

- Stop driving by "your old place" where the two of you used to hang out.

- Delete them from your social networking circle. This includes email addresses, friends' lists, and group contacts.

- Meditate and focus on the peaceful and composed life you now lead without them. (IMPORTANT: When meditating, do not allow your thoughts to drift into the drama that you endured during the relationship. That will only draw more dramatic situations to you. Only focus on the life you desire.)

BE THE BIRD

One gloomy afternoon while I was waiting in the waiting room of my doctor's office, I was in a particularly listless mood and in an attempt to lift my spirits, I picked up an art magazine. I thumbed through it glancing at the images of what appeared to be an array of emotional depictions: pain, glee, impartialness, and joy. I stopped at one piece of artwork and couldn't take my eyes away from it. It was a drawing of a bird sitting atop a perch singing, laughing, and whistling. It was surrounded by blue skies, other birds were flying free, the trees and grass were thick and green, children were playing, and the clouds were fluffy and white. Directly next to the picture was another drawing of what appeared to be the same bird. It was still sitting atop a perch, but the background scene was much different. The skies were almost black, the grass was brown and dead, there were no other signs of

175

life, the wind was howling so hard that the leafless tree branches were nearly about to fall from the bark of the trees. But despite the disturbing background, the bird was still singing, laughing, and whistling. The caption under the first drawing read, "This is not peace…" The caption under the disturbing illustration read, "*This* is peace."

The bird represents the vibrant, deserving, and resilient being that's already within you. It's enjoying the ride even though it gets bumpy. It's aware of the trauma and unsettling atmosphere that has tried to smother and distract her, but she chooses to draw strength from that place of resilience, calm, and unwavering faith so she **can** sing, laugh and whistle despite the iniquities that have tried to consume her.

THIS is what being unstoppable is all about. When you're in the midst of drama, altercations, misfortune, and adversity, and you're still able to find peace, you have truly arrived at being unstoppable. But being unstoppable does not mean you're invincible. Unfortunate things are going to happen, plans will come undone, and unforeseen events will shake you to the core, but when these things happen (and they will), I say to you my friends, "Be the Bird!"

So I will end this chapter the same way it started: "Just who do you think you are?" And your answer is simple…

Unstoppable!

WTF

Women Thriving Fearlessly!

<u>Sponsorship, Press, & Meeting Planners Contact:</u>

430 E. 162nd St #330

South Holland, IL 60473

866-443-6769

info@theunstoppablewoman.net

www.TheUnstoppableWoman.net

Book Erika to teach any content
from this book live!

Made in the USA
Lexington, KY
21 September 2017